362.880 Vio
Violence against women /
$32.00   ocn920683244

3 4028 08851 7686
HARRIS COUNTY PUBLIC LIBRARY

DISCARD

Violence Against Women

D1157130

Other Books in the Current Controversies Series

Violence Against Women

Noël Merino, Book Editor

GREENHAVEN PRESS
A part of Gale, Cengage Learning

GALE
CENGAGE Learning·

Farmington Hills, Mich • San Francisco • New York • Waterville, Maine
Meriden, Conn • Mason, Ohio • Chicago

Judy Galens, *Manager, Frontlist Acquisitions*

© 2016 Greenhaven Press, a part of Gale, Cengage Learning

Gale and Greenhaven Press are registered trademarks used herein under license.

For more information, contact:
Greenhaven Press
27500 Drake Rd.
Farmington Hills, MI 48331-3535
Or you can visit our Internet site at gale.cengage.com

ALL RIGHTS RESERVED.
No part of this work covered by the copyright herein may be reproduced, transmitted, stored, or used in any form or by any means graphic, electronic, or mechanical, including but not limited to photocopying, recording, scanning, digitizing, taping, Web distribution, information networks, or information storage and retrieval systems, except as permitted under Section 107 or 108 of the 1976 United States Copyright Act, without the prior written permission of the publisher.

For product information and technology assistance, contact us at

Gale Customer Support, 1-800-877-4253
For permission to use material from this text or product, submit all requests online at www.cengage.com/permissions

Further permissions questions can be emailed to permissionrequest@cengage.com

Articles in Greenhaven Press anthologies are often edited for length to meet page requirements. In addition, original titles of these works are changed to clearly present the main thesis and to explicitly indicate the author's opinion. Every effort is made to ensure that Greenhaven Press accurately reflects the original intent of the authors. Every effort has been made to trace the owners of copyrighted material.

Cover image © Ron Zmiri/Shutterstock.com.

LIBRARY OF CONGRESS CATALOGING-IN-PUBLICATION DATA

Violence against women (Greenhaven Press) / Violence against women / Noël Merino, Book Editor.
    pages cm. -- (Current controversies)
    Includes bibliographical references and index.
    ISBN 978-0-7377-7426-9 (hardcover) -- ISBN 978-0-7377-7427-6 (pbk.)
    1. Women--Violence against--United States. 2. Women--Crimes against--United States. I. Merino, Noël, editor. II. Title.
    HV6250.4.W65V52153 2016
    362.88082'0973--dc23
                                     2015024205

Printed in the United States of America
1 2 3 4 5   19 18 17 16 15

Contents

Chapter 3: Has Legislation to Reduce Violence Against Women Been Effective?

The 2013 reauthorization bill of the Violence Against Women Act—Senate bill S. 1925—skews the intent of the original 1994 VAWA by adding provisions to protect men, prisoners, and transgender people, which is outside the scope of the original law. S. 1925 also duplicates many services and programs already administered by other federal agencies.

Chapter 4: What Is the Extent of Violence Against Women Worldwide?

Foreword

By definition, controversies are "discussions of questions in which opposing opinions clash" (*Webster's Twentieth Century Dictionary Unabridged*). Few would deny that controversies are a pervasive part of the human condition and exist on virtually every level of human enterprise. Controversies transpire between individuals and among groups, within nations and between nations. Controversies supply the grist necessary for progress by providing challenges and challengers to the status quo. They also create atmospheres where strife and warfare can flourish. A world without controversies would be a peaceful world; but it also would be, by and large, static and prosaic.

The Series' Purpose

The purpose of the Current Controversies series is to explore many of the social, political, and economic controversies dominating the national and international scenes today. Titles selected for inclusion in the series are highly focused and specific. For example, from the larger category of criminal justice, Current Controversies deals with specific topics such as police brutality, gun control, white collar crime, and others. The debates in Current Controversies also are presented in a useful, timeless fashion. Articles and book excerpts included in each title are selected if they contribute valuable, long-range ideas to the overall debate. And wherever possible, current information is enhanced with historical documents and other relevant materials. Thus, while individual titles are current in focus, every effort is made to ensure that they will not become quickly outdated. Books in the Current Controversies series will remain important resources for librarians, teachers, and students for many years.

In addition to keeping the titles focused and specific, great care is taken in the editorial format of each book in the series. Book introductions and chapter prefaces are offered to provide background material for readers. Chapters are organized around several key questions that are answered with diverse opinions representing all points on the political spectrum. Materials in each chapter include opinions in which authors clearly disagree as well as alternative opinions in which authors may agree on a broader issue but disagree on the possible solutions. In this way, the content of each volume in Current Controversies mirrors the mosaic of opinions encountered in society. Readers will quickly realize that there are many viable answers to these complex issues. By questioning each author's conclusions, students and casual readers can begin to develop the critical thinking skills so important to evaluating opinionated material.

Current Controversies is also ideal for controlled research. Each anthology in the series is composed of primary sources taken from a wide gamut of informational categories including periodicals, newspapers, books, US and foreign government documents, and the publications of private and public organizations. Readers will find factual support for reports, debates, and research papers covering all areas of important issues. In addition, an annotated table of contents, an index, a book and periodical bibliography, and a list of organizations to contact are included in each book to expedite further research.

Perhaps more than ever before in history, people are confronted with diverse and contradictory information. During the Persian Gulf War, for example, the public was not only treated to minute-to-minute coverage of the war, it was also inundated with critiques of the coverage and countless analyses of the factors motivating US involvement. Being able to sort through the plethora of opinions accompanying today's major issues, and to draw one's own conclusions, can be a complicated and frustrating struggle. It is the editors' hope that Current Controversies will help readers with this struggle.

Introduction

"Looking at the different rates of domestic violence and sexual violence around the world illustrates that although rates vary worldwide, the problem exists everywhere."

In 2008, United Nations Secretary-General Ban Ki-moon stated, "There is one universal truth, applicable to all countries, cultures and communities: violence against women is never acceptable, never excusable, never tolerable." Yet, all over the world women experience various kinds of violence. In its 2013 report, *Global and Regional Estimates of Violence Against Women: Prevalence and Health Effects of Intimate Partner Violence and Non-Partner Sexual Violence*, the World Health Organization (WHO) notes, "The variation in the prevalence of violence seen within and between communities, countries and regions highlights that violence is not inevitable, and that it can be prevented."[1] Looking at the different rates of domestic violence and sexual violence around the world illustrates that although rates vary worldwide, the problem exists everywhere.

WHO compiled data on the rates of intimate partner violence and nonpartner sexual violence according to the following definitions. WHO defines intimate partner violence as self-reported experience of one or more acts of physical and/or sexual violence by a current or former partner since the age of fifteen years old. Physical violence is defined as:

- Being slapped or having something thrown at you that could hurt you, being pushed or shoved, being hit with

---

1. World Health Organization, *Global and Regional Estimates of Violence Against Women: Prevalence and Health Effects of Intimate Partner Violence and Non-Partner Sexual Violence*, 2013. http://apps.who.int/iris/bitstream/10665/85239/1/9789241564625_eng.pdf?ua =1.

a fist or something else that could hurt, being kicked, dragged or beaten up, being choked or burnt on purpose, and/or being threatened with, or actually, having a gun, knife or other weapon used on you.

Sexual violence is defined as:

- Being physically forced to have sexual intercourse when you did not want to, having sexual intercourse because you were afraid of what your partner might do, and/or being forced to do something sexual that you found humiliating or degrading.

WHO defines nonpartner sexual violence in the following way: "When aged 15 years or over, experience of being forced to perform any sexual act that you did not want to by someone other than your husband/partner."[2]

The data compiled by WHO show that lifetime prevalence of physical or sexual violence by an intimate partner is lower in high-income regions. WHO claims that in the high-income regions of North America, Western Europe, Australia, New Zealand, and Japan, 23.2 percent of women report physical or sexual violence by a partner at some point in their lives. In low- and middle-income regions, however, the percentages are significantly higher: Southeast Asia has the highest rate of women reporting partner violence, at 37.7 percent, with the Eastern Mediterranean and Africa not far behind, at 37.0 and 36.6 percent, respectively. In Central and South America, 29.8 percent of women reported violence from partners, in Eastern Europe 25.4 percent of women reported violence from partners, and in the Western Pacific 24.6 percent of women reported violence from partners, nearly the same rate as in high-income regions.

The data compiled by WHO are reversed, however, when it comes to nonpartner sexual violence. The lifetime prevalence of nonpartner sexual violence is higher in high-income

2. Ibid.

regions than in low- and middle-income regions. In the high-income regions of North America, Western Europe, Australia, New Zealand, and Japan, 12.6 percent of women reported that they had experienced nonpartner sexual violence at some point in their lives. Women in Africa reported the occurrence of such violence at almost the same rate, 11.9 percent, as did women in Central and South America, at 10.7 percent. But only 5.2 percent of women in Eastern Europe reported such violence and only 4.9 percent of women in Southeast Asia reported an occurrence of nonpartner sexual violence.

According to WHO, over one-third of women globally have experienced either intimate partner violence or nonpartner sexual violence. In addition, over one-third of murders of women are committed by intimate partners. WHO found that physical and sexual violence led to other harms beyond the immediate harm of violence: women who experience partner violence are twice as likely to be depressed and have a 16 percent greater odds of having a low-birth-weight baby compared to women who have not experienced such violence.

Violence against women is clearly an issue that affects a large proportion of women worldwide. The authors of the viewpoints in *Current Controversies: Violence Against Women* consider the scope of the problem of violence against women in the United States and explore where violence against women is problematic worldwide. Competing viewpoints are considered on the various causes of violence against women. In addition, various experts weigh in on the issue of the effectiveness of legislation, such as the Violence Against Women Act in the United States. The opinions expressed by these commentators, politicians, and experts on these issues and others in this volume help to shed light on this ongoing social problem.

CHAPTER 1

Is Violence Against Women in the United States a Serious Problem?

Overview: Sexual Violence by Gender and Race

Matthew J. Breiding et al.

Matthew J. Breiding wrote the following viewpoint along with Sharon G. Smith, Kathleen C. Basile, Mikel L. Walters, Jieru Chen, and Melissa T. Merrick. The authors are all researchers at the Centers for Disease Control and Prevention, Division of Violence Prevention.

In the United States, an estimated 19.3% of women (or >23 million women) have been raped during their lifetimes. Completed forced penetration was experienced by an estimated 11.5% of women. Nationally, an estimated 1.6% of women (or approximately 1.9 million women) were raped in the 12 months before taking the survey.

Prevalence of Sexual Violence Victimization

An estimated 1.7% of men (or almost 2.0 million men) were raped during their lifetimes; 0.7% of men experienced completed forced penetration. The case count for men reporting rape in the preceding 12 months was too small to produce a statistically reliable prevalence estimate.

An estimated 43.9% of women experienced sexual violence other than rape during their lifetimes, and an estimated 5.5% of women were victims of sexual violence other than rape in the 12 months preceding the survey. For men, an estimated 23.4% experienced sexual violence other than rape during their lifetimes, and 5.1% experienced sexual violence other than rape in the 12 months before completing the survey.

Matthew J. Breiding, Sharon G. Smith, Kathleen C. Basile, Mikel L. Walters, Jieru Chen, and Melissa T. Merrick, "Prevalence and Characteristics of Sexual Violence, Stalking, and Intimate Partner Violence Victimization—National Intimate Partner and Sexual Violence Survey, United States, 2011," *Morbidity and Mortality Weekly Report*, vol. 63, no. 8, September 5, 2014, pp. 4–6, 9–11. Courtesy Centers for Disease Control and Prevention.

An estimated 0.6% of women (>700,000 women) were made to penetrate a perpetrator during their lifetimes. The case count for women reporting being made to penetrate a perpetrator in the preceding 12 months was too small to produce a statistically reliable prevalence estimate. For men, the lifetime prevalence of being made to penetrate a perpetrator was an estimated 6.7% (>7.6 million men), while an estimated 1.7% of men were made to penetrate a perpetrator in the 12 months preceding the survey. An estimated 12.5% of women experienced sexual coercion during their lifetimes. Sexual coercion was experienced by an estimated 2.0% of women in the 12 months before taking the survey. An estimated 5.8% of men experienced sexual coercion during their lifetimes while an estimated 1.3% of men experienced sexual coercion in the 12 months before taking the survey.

In the United States, an estimated 32.3% of multiracial women, 27.5% of American Indian/Alaska Native women, 21.2% of non-Hispanic black women, 20.5% of non-Hispanic white women, and 13.6% of Hispanic women were raped during their lifetimes.

Approximately one in four women (27.3%) is estimated to have experienced some form of unwanted sexual contact during their lifetimes. In the 12 months preceding the survey, an estimated 2.2% of women experienced unwanted sexual contact. An estimated 10.8% of men experienced unwanted sexual contact during their lifetimes, with an estimated 1.6% of men having experienced unwanted sexual contact in the 12 months before taking the survey.

Approximately one in three women (32.1%) is estimated to have experienced some type of noncontact unwanted sexual experience during their lifetimes, and an estimated 3.4% of women experienced this in the 12 months before taking the survey. An estimated 13.3% of men experienced noncontact unwanted sexual experiences during their lifetimes, and an estimated 2.5% of men experienced this type of victimization in the previous 12 months.

Prevalence of Sexual Violence Victimization by Race/Ethnicity

In the United States, an estimated 32.3% of multiracial women, 27.5% of American Indian/Alaska Native women, 21.2% of non-Hispanic black women, 20.5% of non-Hispanic white women, and 13.6% of Hispanic women were raped during their lifetimes. The case counts of other racial/ethnic categories of women were too small to report statistically reliable estimates. Lifetime estimates of rape for men by race/ethnicity were also not statistically reliable for reporting because of a small case count, with one exception: an estimated 1.6% of non-Hispanic white men were raped during their lifetimes.

An estimated 64.1% of multiracial women, 55.0% of American Indian/Alaska Native women, 46.9% of non-Hispanic white women, and 38.2% of non-Hispanic black women experienced sexual violence other than rape during their lifetimes. In addition, an estimated 35.6% of Hispanic women and 31.9% of Asian or Pacific Islander women experienced sexual violence other than rape during their lifetimes.

Among men, an estimated 39.5% of multiracial men experienced sexual violence other than rape during their lifetimes. In addition, 26.6% of Hispanic men, 24.5% of American Indian/Alaska Native men, 24.4% of non-Hispanic black men, and 22.2% of non-Hispanic white men experienced sexual violence other than rape during their lifetimes, and an estimated 15.8% of Asian or Pacific Islander men experienced this type of sexual violence during their lifetimes.

Characteristics of Sexual Violence Perpetrators

For female rape victims, an estimated 99.0% had only male perpetrators. In addition, an estimated 94.7% of female victims of sexual violence other than rape had only male perpetrators. For male victims, the sex of the perpetrator varied by the type of sexual violence experienced. The majority of male rape victims (an estimated 79.3%) had only male perpetrators. For three of the other forms of sexual violence, a majority of male victims had only female perpetrators: being made to penetrate (an estimated 82.6%), sexual coercion (an estimated 80.0%), and unwanted sexual contact (an estimated 54.7%). For noncontact unwanted sexual experiences, nearly half of male victims (an estimated 46.0%) had only male perpetrators and an estimated 43.6% had only female perpetrators.

The majority of male victims of sexual coercion (an estimated 69.5%) had an intimate partner as a perpetrator.

The majority of victims of all types of sexual violence knew their perpetrators. Almost half of female victims of rape (an estimated 46.7%) had at least one perpetrator who was an acquaintance, and an estimated 45.4% of female rape victims had at least one perpetrator who was an intimate partner. More than half (an estimated 58.4%) of women who experienced alcohol/drug facilitated penetration were victimized by an acquaintance. An estimated 44.9% of male victims of rape were raped by an acquaintance, and an estimated 29.0% of male victims of rape were raped by an intimate partner. The estimates for male victims raped by other types of perpetrators are not reported because the case counts were too small to calculate a reliable estimate.

For sexual violence other than rape of both women and men, the type of perpetrator varied by the form of sexual violence experienced. The majority of female victims of sexual coercion (an estimated 74.1%) had an intimate partner as a perpetrator, and nearly half of female victims of unwanted sexual contact (an estimated 47.2%) had an acquaintance as a perpetrator. About half of the female victims of noncontact unwanted sexual experiences had a stranger as a perpetrator (an estimated 49.3%).

Among men who were made to penetrate a perpetrator, an estimated 54.5% were made to penetrate an intimate partner and an estimated 43.0% were made to penetrate an acquaintance. The majority of male victims of sexual coercion (an estimated 69.5%) had an intimate partner as a perpetrator. Among male victims of unwanted sexual contact, about half (an estimated 51.8%) had an acquaintance as a perpetrator. Finally, among male victims of noncontact unwanted sexual violence, an estimated 39.2% had an acquaintance as a perpetrator, followed by an intimate partner (an estimated 30.9%), or a stranger (an estimated 30.9%). . . .

Prevalence of Intimate Partner Violence Victimization

The lifetime and 12-month prevalence of rape by an intimate partner for women was an estimated 8.8% and 0.8%, respectively. Nationally, an estimated 15.8% of women experienced other forms of sexual violence by an intimate partner during their lifetimes, while an estimated 2.1% of women experienced other forms of sexual violence by a partner in the 12 months before taking the survey. The lifetime prevalence of physical violence by an intimate partner was an estimated 31.5% among women and in the 12 months before taking the survey, an estimated 4.0% of women experienced some form of physical violence by an intimate partner. An estimated 22.3% of women experienced at least one act of severe physical violence by an intimate partner during their lifetimes. With respect to individual severe physical violence behaviors, being slammed against something was experienced by an estimated 15.4% of women, and being hit with a fist or something hard was experienced by 13.2% of women. In the 12 months before taking the survey, an estimated 2.3% of women experienced at least one form of severe physical violence by an intimate partner. The lifetime and 12-month prevalence of stalking by an intimate partner for women was an estimated 9.2% and 2.4%, respectively. Finally, an estimated 47.1% of women experienced at least one act of psychological aggression by an intimate partner during their lifetimes; an estimated 14.2% of women experienced some form of psychological aggression in the 12 months preceding the survey.

An estimated 26.8% of multiracial women, 17.4% of non-Hispanic black women, 17.1% of non-Hispanic white women, and 9.9% of Hispanic women experienced sexual violence other than rape by an intimate partner during their lifetimes.

Nationally, an estimated 0.5% of men experienced rape by an intimate partner during their lifetimes. However, the case count for men reporting rape by an intimate partner in the preceding 12 months was too small to produce a statistically reliable prevalence estimate. An estimated 9.5% of men experienced other forms of sexual violence by an intimate partner during their lifetimes, while an estimated 2.1% of men experienced other forms of sexual violence by an intimate partner in the 12 months before taking the survey. The lifetime prevalence of physical violence by an intimate partner was an estimated 27.5% for men, and in the 12 months before taking the survey, an estimated 4.8% of men experienced some form of physical violence by an intimate partner. An estimated 14.0% of men experienced at least one act of severe physical violence by an intimate partner during their lifetimes. With respect to individual severe physical violence behaviors, being hit with a fist or something hard was experienced by an estimated 10.1% of men, and 4.6% of men have been kicked by an intimate partner. In the 12 months before taking the survey, an estimated 2.1% of men experienced at least one form of severe physical violence by an intimate partner. The lifetime and 12-month prevalence of stalking by an intimate partner for men was an estimated 2.5% and 0.8%, respectively. Finally, an estimated 46.5% of men experienced at least one act of psychological aggression by an intimate partner during their lifetimes; an estimated 18.0% of men experienced some form of psychological aggression in the 12 months preceding the survey.

Prevalence of Intimate Partner Violence Victimization by Race/Ethnicity

Nationally, an estimated 11.4% of multiracial women, 9.6% of non-Hispanic white women, 8.8% of non-Hispanic black women, and 6.2% of Hispanic women were raped by an intimate partner during their lifetimes. The case counts for men reporting rape by an intimate partner during their lifetimes were too small to produce statistically reliable prevalence estimates by race/ethnicity.

An estimated 26.8% of multiracial women, 17.4% of non-Hispanic black women, 17.1% of non-Hispanic white women, and 9.9% of Hispanic women experienced sexual violence other than rape by an intimate partner during their lifetimes. The case counts of other female racial/ethnic groups (Asian or Pacific Islander and American Indian/Alaska Native) were too small to report statistically reliable estimates. In addition, an estimated 18.2% of multiracial men, 14.8% of non-Hispanic black men, 13.5% of Hispanic men, and 7.6% of non-Hispanic white men experienced sexual violence other than rape by an intimate partner at some point during their lifetimes. The case counts of other male racial/ethnic groups (Asian or Pacific Islander and American Indian/Alaska Native) were too small to report statistically reliable estimates.

An estimated 51.7% of American Indian/Alaska Native women, 51.3% of multiracial women, 41.2% of non-Hispanic black women, 30.5% of non-Hispanic white women, 29.7% of

Hispanic women, and 15.3% of Asian or Pacific Islander women experienced physical violence by an intimate partner during their lifetimes. An estimated 43.0% of American Indian/Alaska Native men, 39.3% of multiracial men, 36.3% of non-Hispanic black men, 27.1% of Hispanic men, 26.6% of non-Hispanic white men, and 11.5% of Asian or Pacific Islander men experienced physical violence by an intimate partner during their lifetime.

An estimated 13.3% of multiracial women, 9.9% of non-Hispanic white women, 9.5% of non-Hispanic black women, and 6.8% of Hispanic women were stalked by an intimate partner during their lifetimes. The case counts of other female racial/ethnic groups (Asian or Pacific Islander and American Indian/Alaska Native) were too small to report statistically reliable estimates.

In addition, an estimated 1.7% of non-Hispanic white men were stalked by an intimate partner during their lifetimes. The case counts of all other male racial/ethnic groups were too small to report statistically reliable estimates.

Violence Against Women Is a Major Public Policy Issue

Office on Violence Against Women

The Office on Violence Against Women, a component of the US Department of Justice, was created in 1995 to help facilitate programs under the Violence Against Women Act.

Over the past 35 years, violence against women has become recognized as a major public policy issue in this country. The violence may be perpetrated by those closest to the victim/survivor or by a total stranger, and it encompasses a continuum of crimes and related behaviors that include sexual assault, domestic violence, dating violence, and stalking. It is not uncommon for victims/survivors to experience more than one type of victimization or to be victimized by multiple perpetrators over their lifetime. Violence against women rarely consists of one-time occurrences, but rather comprises clusters of behavior that are ongoing and repetitive. The violence is generally purposeful, designed to coerce, entrap, and subordinate victims and to engender fear in them. It harms the body and spirit, and may result in protracted recovery or permanent injuries. The economic costs are often far-reaching, and victims rarely receive even partial reparations. The adverse effects of this violence ripple well beyond the victim/survivor herself, expanding to her children and other family members, her workplace, and her community and impacting all sectors and institutions of society.

Domestic Violence and Dating Violence

It is estimated that more than 42 million women in the United States will experience physical violence, rape, and/or stalking by an intimate partner during their lifetime. As many as 1 in

Office on Violence Against Women, "2012 Biennial Report to Congress on the Effectiveness of Grant Programs Under the Violence Against Women Act," US Department of Justice, 2012, pp. 5–8. Courtesy of the US Department of Justice.

3 women experience physical violence, and 1 in 10 will be raped by their intimate partner.

Although both men and women use violence in intimate partnerships, the most severe violence (i.e., involving broken bones, injury to bodily organs, sexual assault or coercion, and strangulation) is overwhelmingly inflicted by men against their women partners. The Centers for Disease Control and Prevention (CDC) recently released the National Intimate Partner and Sexual Violence Survey (NISVS), a key study that estimates the prevalence of sexual assault, intimate partner violence, and stalking, based on 16,507 interviews with men and women in the United States. According to this study, approximately 1 in 4 women, compared with 1 in 7 men, have been victims of severe physical violence by an intimate partner. In 2010, 1,095 women were killed by their male partners (i.e., current and former husbands and boyfriends) and 241 men were killed by their female partners (i.e., current and former wives and girlfriends) in the U.S.

Of all female victims who had experienced rape ... 51 percent were raped by a current or former intimate partner and 41 percent by an acquaintance.

In addition to domestic violence, dating violence is also reported to occur frequently. As defined by VAWA [Violence Against Women Act] 2005, dating violence includes violence committed by a person who is or has been in a social relationship of a romantic or intimate nature with the victim. An analysis of data from the Youth Risk Behavior Survey found that approximately 10 percent of high school students (10.3 percent of males and 9.3 percent of females) had been hit, slapped, or otherwise physically hurt by their dating partner in the year preceding the survey. A study based on a nationally representative sample of 12- to 17-year-olds found that approximately 413,000 adolescents (335,000 females and

78,000 males) experience severe dating violence each year. Sexual assault and physical violence were the most common forms of violence reported.

Intimate partner violence often begins at a young age. One in 5 women and 1 in 7 men who had experienced intimate partner violence were between 11 and 17 years old at the time of their first violent experience. Women age 16 to 24 experience the highest per capita rates of intimate partner violence. Studies of adult women suggest prevalence rates of dating violence victimization ranging from 20 to 37 percent.

The Incidence of Sexual Assault

Sexual assault is any type of sexual contact or behavior that occurs without the explicit consent of the recipient. Falling under the definition of sexual assault are sexual activities such as forced sexual intercourse, forcible sodomy, child molestation, incest, fondling, and attempted rape. Sexual assault is perpetrated in a range of relationships, from strangers, acquaintances, and dating partners to intimate or married partners of the victims/survivors.

The shame and fear experienced by survivors of sexual assault may prevent them from seeking assistance.

According to the NISVS study, approximately 18 percent of women in the United States have experienced rape, 44.6 percent have experienced some other form of sexual violence, and approximately 1 in 10 women has been raped by an intimate partner. Of all female victims who had experienced rape—whether completed, attempted, or alcohol- or drug-facilitated—51 percent were raped by a current or former intimate partner and 41 percent by an acquaintance.

Women younger than 25 are at increased risk for sexual assault. More than 75 percent of women surveyed in the NISVS study who had been victims of a completed rape were first raped before their 25th birthday, with approximately 42 percent of these victims experiencing their first completed rape before the age of 18.

A large number of 18- to 25-year-old women reside on college campuses, and researchers have studied this population to determine the prevalence of violence and associated factors. A longitudinal study examining prevalence rates among high school and college women found that between adolescence and their fourth year of college, 79 percent of respondents reported experiencing sexual victimization, which was defined as "unwanted contact," "verbal coercion," "attempted rape," or "rape." A study of undergraduate students revealed that 22 percent had experienced a sexual assault following a stalking incident. The Campus Sexual Assault (CSA) Study surveyed more than 6,800 undergraduate students in two large public universities and found that of the 5,466 women who completed the survey, 13.7 percent had been victims of at least one completed sexual assault since entering college. Just under 5 percent of these young women were physically forced, and approximately 8 percent were incapacitated and unable to consent, having either voluntarily consumed alcohol or drugs or been involuntarily drugged. The Historically Black College and University Campus Sexual Assault (HBCU CSA) Study, which assessed multiple factors related to sexual assault on four Historically Black College and University (HBCU) campuses, found that approximately 10 percent of the 3,951 undergraduate women surveyed had experienced a completed sexual assault since entering college.

The Impact of Sexual Assault

Sexual assault impacts victims/survivors on many levels and in many ways. Physical injuries and emotional and psychological challenges such as shame, guilt, and fear are common. The National Violence Against Women Survey found that during their lifetime, nearly 18 million women and 3 million men had experienced a sexual assault, and almost a third of the women sustained physical injury as a result of the sexual assault. Studies of intimate partner sexual assault demonstrate significantly greater prevalence of post-traumatic stress disorder, stress, and dissociation in victims/survivors when compared with non-intimate-partner sexual assaults and non-sexual physical assault of women. A 4-year study of 352 women ages 14 to 65 who visited an emergency room after a sexual assault found that 76 percent of the women knew their offender, either as an intimate partner or as an acquaintance or a recently met acquaintance; 24 percent reported the perpetrator to be a stranger. The rates of any type of physical injury reported were higher among women assaulted by an intimate partner. Further, women in intimate relationships with their abusers are less likely to seek services and are at greater risk for further sexual abuse when they try to leave the relationship.

Studies of cyberstalking prevalence among college students reveal incidence rates between 3 and 41 percent for various forms of cyberstalking.

The shame and fear experienced by survivors of sexual assault may prevent them from seeking assistance. In a study of 215 college students (55 percent of whom were female), the most crucial barriers reported were shame and guilt, issues of confidentiality, fear of retaliation, and worry about not being believed. For these and other reasons, sexual assault survivors do not always seek assistance from the very systems set up to help them. A study of more than 3,000 women between the ages of 18 and 86 suggests a lifetime prevalence rate of sexual assault as high as 18 percent for the 112 million women living in the U.S., with only 1 in 5 women reporting their victimization to the police. Only 37 percent of cases were prosecuted after they were reported to law enforcement.

The Problem of Stalking

Findings from NISVS show that approximately 1 in 6 women (16.2 percent) and 1 in 19 men (5.2 percent) in the United States have experienced stalking. Although the general public is most familiar with stalking by strangers, the majority of stalking is perpetrated by partners or former partners of the stalking victims, or other people known to the victims. Females are at greater risk of being stalked by an intimate partner than are men, with two-thirds (66.2 percent) of women reporting being victimized by a current or former partner, and 41.4 percent of men reporting the same. The rates of stalking victimization by a stranger are 13.2 percent for women and 19 percent for men. Research suggests that those who stalk in the context of a romantic relationship are more violent and threatening to their victims both physically and emotionally than non-partner stalkers. Although 80 to 90 percent of victims report that partner stalking begins during the relationship, about half of these victims are stalked by proxies for their intimate partners. Partner stalking is commonplace in protection order violations. Stalking is not a singular act. Among stalking victims, almost half (46 percent) report at least one unwanted contact per week and 11 percent report that they have been stalked for 5 years or more.

A variety of tactics are used against stalking victims, including unwanted phone calls, voice and text messages, and hang-ups. NISVS indicates that 78.8 percent of female victims have experienced such actions, and more than half (57.6 percent) reported being approached by their stalkers. Additionally, nearly 40 percent were watched, followed, or tracked by some form of technology. Stalking has been associated with a range of serious consequences for victims, including increased risk of violence, injury, and homicide. An analysis of 54 studies estimated that threats are used in 54 percent of stalking cases; another analysis of 82 studies indicated the use of physical violence in 32 percent and sexual violence in 12 percent of stalking cases.

Stalking traditionally takes the form of unwanted direct and/or indirect contact, but now 26 percent of stalking victims experience cyberstalking—unwanted contact or monitoring through electronic devices—according to respondents from the National Crime Victimization Survey. The accelerated development and availability of communication technology, combined with the under-reporting of stalking crimes in general, means that the actual number of cyberstalking victims is likely to be much higher. Studies of cyberstalking prevalence among college students reveal incidence rates between 3 and 41 percent for various forms of cyberstalking and suggest that college students are at greater risk of cyberstalking victimization than the general population. Cyberstalking shares the fundamentals of traditional stalking and leads to many of the same consequences for victims as discussed above.

Domestic Violence Is a Problem That Deserves More Attention

Doug Pardue et al.

Doug Pardue wrote the following viewpoint along with Glenn Smith, Jennifer Berry Hawes, and Natalie Caula Hauff. The authors are investigative journalists for The Post and Courier *in Charleston, South Carolina.*

More than 300 women were shot, stabbed, strangled, beaten, bludgeoned or burned to death over the past decade by men in South Carolina, dying at a rate of one every 12 days while the state does little to stem the carnage from domestic abuse.

Violence Against Women in South Carolina

More than three times as many women have died here at the hands of current or former lovers than the number of Palmetto State soldiers killed in the Iraq and Afghanistan wars combined.

It's a staggering toll that for more than 15 years has placed South Carolina among the top 10 states nationally in the rate of women killed by men. The state topped the list on three occasions, including this past year [2013], when it posted a murder rate for women that was more than double the national rate.

Awash in guns, saddled with ineffective laws and lacking enough shelters for the battered, South Carolina is a state where the deck is stacked against women trapped in the cycle of abuse, a *Post and Courier* investigation has found.

Doug Pardue, Glenn Smith, Jennifer Berry Hawes, and Natalie Caula Hauff, "Till Death Do Us Part: Part One," *The Post and Courier* (Charleston, SC), August 19, 2014. Copyright © 2014 Post and Courier. All rights reserved. Reproduced with permission.

Couple this with deep-rooted beliefs about the sanctity of marriage and the place of women in the home, and the vows "till death do us part" take on a sinister tone.

A Silent Epidemic

The beat of killings has remained a constant in South Carolina, even as domestic violence rates have tumbled 64 percent nationwide over the past two decades, according to an analysis of crime statistics by the newspaper. This blood has spilled in every corner of the state, from beach towns and mountain hamlets to farming villages and sprawling urban centers, cutting across racial, ethnic and economic lines.

Nationwide, an average of three women are killed by a current or former lover every day.

Consider 25-year-old Erica Olsen of Anderson, who was two months pregnant when her boyfriend stabbed her 25 times in front of her young daughter in October 2006. Or Andrenna Butler, 72, whose estranged husband drove from Pennsylvania to gun her down in her Newberry home in December. Or 30-year-old Dara Watson, whose fiancé shot her in the head at their Mount Pleasant home and dumped her in a Lowcountry forest in February 2012 before killing himself.

Interviews with more than 100 victims, counselors, police, prosecutors and judges reveal an ingrained, multi-generational problem in South Carolina, where abusive behavior is passed down from parents to their children. Yet the problem essentially remains a silent epidemic, a private matter that is seldom discussed outside the home until someone is seriously hurt.

"We have the notion that what goes on between a couple is just between the couple and is none of our business," said 9th Circuit Solicitor Scarlett Wilson, chief prosecutor for Charleston and Berkeley counties. "Where that analysis goes wrong is we have to remember that couple is training their little boy that this is how he treats women and training their little girl that this is what she should expect from her man. The cycle is just perpetual."

A Lack of Action

South Carolina is hardly alone in dealing with domestic violence. Nationwide, an average of three women are killed by a current or former lover every day. Other states are moving forward with reform measures, but South Carolina has largely remained idle while its domestic murder rate consistently ranks among the nation's worst.

Though state officials have long lamented the high death toll for women, lawmakers have put little money into prevention programs and have resisted efforts to toughen penalties for abusers. This past year alone, a dozen measures to combat domestic violence died in the Legislature.

The state's largest metro areas of Greenville, Columbia and Charleston lead the death tally in sheer numbers. But rural pockets, such as Marlboro, Allendale and Greenwood counties, hold more danger because the odds are higher there that a woman will die from domestic violence. These are places where resources for victims of abuse are thin, a predicament the state has done little to address.

All 46 counties have at least one animal shelter to care for stray dogs and cats, but the state has only 18 domestic violence shelters to help women trying to escape abuse in the home. Experts say that just isn't enough in a state that records around 36,000 incidents of domestic abuse every year. More than 380 victims were turned away from shelters around the state between 2012 and 2013 because they had no room, according to the state Department of Social Services.

Oconee County, in South Carolina's rural northwest corner, realized it had a problem last year after six people died over six months in domestic killings. The sheriff pushed for the county to open a shelter after 58-year-old Gwendolyn Hiott was shot dead while trying to leave her husband, who then killed himself. She had nowhere to go, but the couple's 24 cats and dogs were taken to the local animal shelter to be fed and housed while waiting for adoption.

Studies have shown that the risk of being killed by an angry lover declines three months after separation and drops sharply after a year's time.

When asked, most state legislators profess deep concern over domestic violence. Yet they maintain a legal system in which a man can earn five years in prison for abusing his dog but a maximum of just 30 days in jail for beating his wife or girlfriend on a first offense.

Many states have harsher penalties. Mississippi, Ohio and Tennessee, for example, set the maximum jail stay for the same crime at six months. In Georgia and Alabama it is a year.

This extra time behind bars not only serves as a deterrent but also can save lives, according to counselors, prosecutors and academics. Studies have shown that the risk of being killed by an angry lover declines three months after separation and drops sharply after a year's time.

Wife Beaters Get Lenient Treatment

More than a third of those charged in South Carolina domestic killings over the past decade had at least one prior arrest for criminal domestic violence or assault. More than 70 percent of those people had multiple prior arrests on those charges, with one man alone charged with a dozen domestic assaults. The majority spent just days in jail as a result of those crimes.

A prime example is Lee Dell Bradley, a 59-year-old Summerville man accused of fatally stabbing his longtime girlfriend, Frances Lawrence, in late May. Despite two prior arrests for violating court orders meant to protect Lawrence, the longest Bradley ever stayed in jail for abusing women was 81 days. And that came only after he appeared before a judge on a domestic violence charge for the fifth time.

Then there is 55-year-old David Reagan of Charleston, who spent less than a year in jail total on three previous domestic violence convictions before he was charged with strangling a girlfriend in 2013 while awaiting trial on an earlier domestic violence charge involving the girlfriend.

The *Post and Courier* investigation also found:

- Police and court resources vary wildly across the state. Larger cities, such as Charleston, generally have dedicated police units and special courts to deal with domestic violence. Most small towns do not, making it difficult to track abusers, catch signs of escalating violence and make services readily available to both victims and abusers.

- Accused killers are tunneled into a state court system that struggles with overloaded dockets and depends on plea deals to push cases through. Of those convicted of domestic homicides since 2005, nearly half pleaded guilty to lesser charges that carry lighter sentences.

- Guns were the weapon of choice in nearly seven out of every 10 domestic killings of women over the past decade, but South Carolina lawmakers have blocked efforts to keep firearms out of the hands of abusers. Unlike South Carolina, more than two-thirds of all states bar batterers facing restraining orders from having firearms, and about half of those allow or require police to seize guns when they respond to domestic violence complaints.

- Abusers get out of jail quickly because of low bail requirements. Some states, including Maryland and Con-
  necticut, screen domestic cases to determine which
  offenders pose the most danger to their victims. South
  Carolina doesn't do this.

- Domestic abusers often are diverted to anger-
  management programs rather than jail even though
  many experts agree that they don't work. In Charleston,
  authorities hauled one young man into court in March
  after he failed to complete his anger-management program. His excuse: He had missed his appointments because he had been jailed again for breaking into his
  girlfriend's home and beating her.

- Victims are encouraged to seek orders of protection,
  but the orders lack teeth, and the state has no central
  means to alert police that an order exists. Take the case
  of 46-year-old Robert Irby, who still had the restraining
  order paperwork in his hand the day he confessed to
  stalking and killing his ex-girlfriend in Greer in 2010.
  He gunned her down outside her home the day after
  he learned about the order.

- The vast majority of states have fatality-review teams in
  place that study domestic killings for patterns and lessons that can be used to prevent future violence. South
  Carolina is one of only nine states without such a
  team.

A Political Problem

Located in the heart of the Bible Belt, South Carolina is a
deeply conservative state where men have ruled for centuries.
The state elected its first female governor four years ago, but
men continue to dominate elected offices, judicial appointments and other seats of government and corporate power. In

many respects, the state's power structure is a fraternity reluctant to challenge the belief that a man's home is his castle and what goes on there, stays there.

Even as we have gone up in the number of murders and attempted murders over the years, that support [for domestic violence prevention] has never changed.

"Some of this is rooted in this notion of women as property and maintaining the privacy of what goes on within the walls of the home," said state Rep. Gilda Cobb-Hunter, an Orangeburg Democrat. "And a lot of it has to do with this notion of gun rights as well. When all of those things are rolled into one, it tends to speak to why we rank so high in the number of fatalities."

Against this backdrop, it has often been difficult to get traction for spending more tax dollars for domestic violence programs and bolstering protections for the abused. The only consistent state money spent on such programs comes from a sliver of proceeds from marriage license fees—a figure that has hovered for years around $800,000 for the entire state. That's just a tad more than lawmakers earmarked this year for improvements to a fish farm in Colleton County. It equates to roughly $22 for each domestic violence victim.

"Even as we have gone up in the number of murders and attempted murders over the years, that support has never changed," said Rebecca Williams-Agee, director of prevention and education for the S.C. Coalition Against Domestic Violence and Sexual Assault. "It's all wrapped up in the politics of this state and the stereotypes of domestic violence victims. Why does she stay? Why doesn't she pull herself up by her own bootstraps?"

Alicia Alvarez put up with abuse for years before she got the courage to leave. The Charleston mother of two said abusers create an atmosphere that robs victims of confidence.

Abusers don't begin by hitting or killing, Alvarez said. "It begins with little criticisms, second-guessing everything you do. They get in your brain so that when they tell you, 'You are worthless,' you believe it."

A Failure to Pass Legislation

Just a few months after South Carolina's most recent designation as the deadliest in the nation for women, the state's Legislature took up about a dozen bills aimed at toughening penalties for abusers, keeping guns out of their hands and keeping them away from their victims.

The bills languished in committees and died, with the exception of a lone provision that aims to protect the welfare of family pets left in the care of a person facing domestic abuse charges.

Five of those measures got stuck in the Senate Judiciary Committee, a panel filled with lawyers. Its chairman is Larry Martin, a Republican from Pickens County, where nine domestic killings occurred over the past decade.

Martin wasn't sure why the bills failed to advance, but he stressed that he is a strong supporter of measures to reduce domestic abuse. He said lawmakers had approved meaningful legislation on the topic in recent years and that the measures had a powerful impact, though he couldn't recall what those bills were.

Families are being destroyed by this violence. That shouldn't be acceptable to any of us.

"I promise you there is no effort to hold anything up," he said. "We are generally supportive of legislation that helps reduce the horrible statistics we have each year on domestic violence."

If so, Cobb-Hunter hasn't seen it. She pushed a proposal to require abusers to surrender their firearms if convicted of domestic violence or facing a restraining order. The proposal went nowhere after running headlong into the state's powerful gun lobby in an election year, she said.

"You put those two things together and you see the results—nothing happens. But, at the same time, families are being destroyed by this violence. That shouldn't be acceptable to any of us."

State Rep. Bakari Sellers' proposal to stiffen penalties for first-time domestic violence offenders met a similar fate. The Democrat from Denmark, who is running for lieutenant governor, said some of his fellow House Judiciary Committee members seemed more intent on blaming victims for staying in abusive relationships than in giving the bill a fair airing.

"It's a big issue statewide, but people were just indifferent," Sellers said. "The sad part is that women will die."

After several calls to legislators from *The Post and Courier*, House Speaker Bobby Harrell contacted the newspaper in early June to say he was disappointed the session had ended with no action on domestic violence reform. The Charleston Republican pledged to appoint an ad hoc committee, led by a female lawmaker, to study the issue prior to the next legislative session and chart a path for change. No appointments had been made by Monday, but they were said to be in the works.

This time, Harrell said, things will be different.

Paulette Sullivan Moore, vice president of public policy for Washington, D.C.-based National Network to End Domestic Violence, said curbing domestic violence is possible with good laws and systems for protecting women. But South Carolina's lingering presence among the top states for domestic homicides shows the state isn't getting the job done, she said.

"To be in the top 10 states for so many years is pretty significant," she said. "I think that says the state needs to take advantage of this opportunity to craft good policy and legislation to ensure that it is not failing half of its population."

If history holds true, 30 more women will be dead by the end of the next legislative session in June 2015, when lawmakers have another chance to stem the violence.

All too often in South Carolina, [domestic violence] ends with women paying the ultimate price.

The Thin Line

Every year, people from across South Carolina gather at the Statehouse in Columbia to remember those killed in domestic violence, a somber ceremony marked by the reading of names and tolling of bells.

Politicians, prosecutors and other advocates repeat calls for an end to the bloodshed and proclaim criminal domestic violence the state's No. 1 law enforcement priority.

Poets, scholars and philosophers have long rhapsodized about the thin line separating love from hate, a delicate thread that, when bent, can fuel a ravenous passion for reckoning and retribution. All too often in South Carolina, this ends with women paying the ultimate price.

That was the case just before Christmas 2011, when Avery Blandin, 49, stalked through the front of a Wal-Mart store in suburban Greenville County, seething with rage and carrying a 12-inch knife tucked into the waistband of his slacks.

Built like a fireplug and prone to blowing his stack, Blandin marched into the bank inside the store where his wife Lilia worked and began shouting. He jerked her onto a table and pulled out his knife, stabbing her again and again. When she slumped to the floor, he stomped on her head and neck.

Lilia died within the hour. She was 38.

Blandin had used his wife as a punching bag for years. She had filed charges against him, sought orders of protection and slept in her car to keep him at bay. But none of that stopped him from making good on his threats to kill her that December day.

"I loved her," Blandin told an Upstate courtroom after pleading guilty to her murder. "She was my wife, my best friend."

Rape Culture? It's Too Real

Sally Kohn

Sally Kohn is a CNN contributor and columnist for The Daily Beast.

We don't yet know all the facts behind the now-infamous, poorly fact-checked story in *Rolling Stone* about an alleged gang rape at the University of Virginia. What we do know: *Rolling Stone* at first blamed the alleged victim, "Jackie"—rather than its own journalistic sloppiness—for so-called "discrepancies" (before changing its callous statement).

And new reporting by the *Washington Post* does reveal that Jackie's friends, cited in the story, say they are skeptical about some of the details. Still, they all believe that Jackie experienced something "horrific" that night, in the words of one, and we do know that Jackie stands by her story. Most of the doubts about it were apparently raised by those she's accusing, including the fraternity and main alleged assailant—whom, I guess, we're supposed to believe instead.

The Skepticism About Rape Culture

But one other thing we do know is that gang rapes just like what Jackie is alleging do happen—too often, and all over America. Here's one measure: Today the Department of Justice's Bureau of Justice Statistics released a new report showing that 80% of college rapes and sexual assaults go unreported to police, and 67% of such attacks by non-students go unreported. It would be a terrible and infuriating mistake to use the confusion around Jackie's story as a convenient way to discount this reality.

Sally Kohn, "Rape Culture? It's Too Real," CNN, December 11, 2014. Copyright © 2014 CNN. All rights reserved. Reproduced with permission.

While *Rolling Stone*'s reporting was clearly shoddy, for example, some writers who initially poked holes in Jackie's story did so for ideological motives. For instance, even before the reporting lapses were revealed, conservative commentator Jonah Goldberg called Jackie's story unbelievable. "It is not credible," Goldberg wrote in the *Los Angeles Times*. "I don't believe it."

Whatever the reality of what happened to Jackie, . . . [many people are] skeptical because they simply don't believe rapes like that happen with the participation of groups of assailants, let alone the complicity of bystanders.

Instead, Goldberg insisted, Jackie's account was "a convenient conversation for an exposé of rape culture," something, incidentally, Goldberg also doubts to be real. "'Rape culture' suggests that there is a large and obvious belief system that condones and enables rape as an end in itself in America," Goldberg later wrote in *National Review*. It's all hogwash, says Goldberg, alleging that the very idea of "rape culture" is just "an elaborate political lie intended to strengthen the hand of activists."

In other words, whatever the reality of what happened to Jackie, Goldberg and others were skeptical because they simply don't believe rapes like that happen with the participation of groups of assailants, let alone the complicity of bystanders. This is where they're mistaken.

The Incidence of Gang Rape

On October 24, 2009, in Richmond, California, a 15-year-old girl was repeatedly raped by a group of young men in a courtyard outside their high school homecoming dance. Six assailants were eventually tried and ultimately pleaded guilty or were convicted. Over two hours, as the assault occurred, as many as 20 other people watched. "As people announced over time that this was going on, more people came to see, and some actually participated," said Lt. Mark Gagan of the Richmond Police Department. The witnesses didn't report the crime to police.

On August 12, 2012, a 16-year-old girl who was incapacitated by alcohol was raped by two high school football players in Steubenville, Ohio. In the backseat of a car and later in the basement of a house, the two assailants stripped their victim naked and took turns, one inserting his fingers into her vagina, the other forcing his penis into her mouth. This is not in dispute. Both football players were convicted of the crime.

As the crimes were taking place, friends took pictures that were shared with other friends. Ultimately, Ohio investigators confiscated 17 cell phones used in sharing the pictures. Some of those at the party even posted pictures of the unresponsive girl, being carried by her wrists and ankles, on Twitter with words like "rape" and "drunk girl." In Steubenville, four adults have been indicted after being accused of covering up the incident, including the school superintendent.

What feminists want—as we all should—is a culture in which it is safe for women to report sexual assault when it happens.

On May 11, 2014, an 18-year-old woman was allegedly sexually assaulted by three students at a party after their high school prom. The three alleged assailants, all prominent athletes, have been charged with multiple counts of aggravated assault and are awaiting trial. According to police, at least one person witnessed the assault in the room where it took place and several other people at the party knew it was happening. But no one stopped it.

In June 2014, a 16-year-old girl went to a party where she was allegedly drugged and raped. She doesn't remember what happened, only passing out and waking up the next morning with her clothes messed up. But weeks later, the young woman received text messages of photos showing her unconscious and undressed, apparently taken at the same party. The photos went viral on the Internet, with Twitter users posting photos of themselves in the same awkward position, mocking the alleged victim. When the *Houston Press* asked someone who posted such a picture on Twitter why he did it, he simply said he was "bored at 1 a.m. and decided to wake up" his Twitter feed.

The Need for a Safe Culture

This is by no means an exhaustive account of incidents in which young women have been gang raped while bystanders have either cheered the crime, hidden it or stood by in silence. In the case of Jackie, I believe in innocence until guilt is proven, even as I realize that we have a society where rapists are given the benefit of the doubt, often despite overwhelming evidence, while female victims are shamed (see multiple Bill Cosby allegations).

The fact is, there doesn't appear to be any incentive for Jackie to have lied. She wasn't seeking to tell her story in the first place (the *Rolling Stone* reporter found her), and she must have known that she would face the usual victim shaming and blaming (witness the slime "journalists" who have now published what they allege is Jackie's full name and address). Indeed, while Jackie named the fraternity involved, she left her alleged assailants' names out of it, so it's hard to see what sort of "revenge" agenda could be served by fabrication.

Anti-feminists have it wrong. No one, myself included, wants Jackie's story to be true (that's absurd and offensive), but we cannot apologize for erring on the side of a fair, compassionate and credulous hearing of a woman's account. What feminists want—as we all should—is a culture in which it is safe for women to report sexual assault when it happens, where they can trust that their families, their peers, the police and courts and, yes, the media will respond with sensitivity and compassion, not skepticism and shame.

Domestic Violence Myths Help No One

Christina Hoff Sommers

Christina Hoff Sommers is a resident scholar of the American Enterprise Institute and author of Who Stole Feminism? How Women Have Betrayed Women.

"The facts are clear," said Attorney General Eric Holder. "Intimate partner homicide is the leading cause of death for African-American women ages 15 to 45."

That's a horrifying statistic, and it would be a shocking reflection of the state of the black family, and American society generally, if it were true. But it isn't true.

False Claims About Male Domestic Violence

According to the Centers for Disease Control and Prevention and the Justice Department's own Bureau of Justice Statistics, the leading causes of death for African-American women between the ages 15–45 are cancer, heart disease, unintentional injuries such as car accidents, and HIV disease. Homicide comes in fifth—and includes murders by strangers. In 2006 (the latest year for which full statistics are available), several hundred African-American women died from intimate partner homicide—each one a tragedy and an outrage, but far fewer than the approximately 6,800 women who died of the other leading causes.

Yet Holder's patently false assertion has remained on the Justice Department website for more than a year.

How is that possible? It is possible because false claims about male domestic violence are ubiquitous and immune to

Christina Hoff Sommers, "Domestic Violence Myths Help No One," *USA Today*, February 4, 2011. Copyright © 2011 USA Today. All rights reserved. Reproduced with permission.

refutation. During the era of the infamous Super Bowl Hoax, it was widely believed that on Super Bowl Sundays, violence against women increases 40%. Journalists began to refer to the game as the "abuse bowl" and quoted experts who explained how male viewers, intoxicated and pumped up with testosterone, could "explode like mad linemen." During the 1993 Super Bowl, NBC ran a public service announcement warning men they would go to jail for attacking their wives.

Those who promulgate false statistics about domestic violence, however well-meaning, promote prejudice.

In this roiling sea of media credulity, one lone journalist, *Washington Post* reporter Ken Ringle, checked the facts. As it turned out, there was no source: An activist had misunderstood something she read, jumped to her sensational conclusion, announced it at a news conference and an urban myth was born. Despite occasional efforts to prove the story true, no one has ever managed to link the Super Bowl to domestic battery.

The So-Called World Cup Abuse

Yet the story has proved too politically convenient to kill off altogether. Last summer, it came back to life on a different continent and with a new accent. During the 2010 World Cup, British newspapers carried stories with headlines such as "Women's World Cup Abuse Nightmare" and informed women that the games could uncover "for the first time, a darker side to their partner." Fortunately, a BBC program called *Law in Action* took the unusual route pioneered by Ringle: The news people actually checked the facts. Their conclusion: a stunt based on cherry-picked figures.

But when the BBC journalists presented the deputy chief constable, Carmel Napier, from the town of Gwent with evidence that the World Cup abuse campaign was based on twisted statistics, she replied: "If it has saved lives, then it is worth it."

It is not worth it. Misinformation leads to misdirected policies that fail to target the true causes of violence. Worse, those who promulgate false statistics about domestic violence, however well-meaning, promote prejudice. Most of the exaggerated claims implicate the average male in a social atrocity. Why do that? Anti-male misandry, like anti-female misogyny, is unjust and dangerous. Recall what happened at Duke University a few years ago when many seemingly fair-minded students and faculty stood by and said nothing while three innocent young men on the Duke Lacrosse team were subjected to the horrors of a modern-day witch hunt.

A False Moral Equivalence

Worst of all, misinformation about violence against women suggests a false moral equivalence between societies where women are protected by law and those where they are not. American and British societies are not perfect, but we have long ago decided that violence against women is barbaric. By contrast, the Islamic Republic of Iran—where it is legal to bury an adulterous woman up to her neck and stone her— was last year granted a seat on the United Nations Commission on the Status of Women. Iranian President Mahmoud Ahmadinejad defended the decision by noting Iranian women are far better off than women in the West. "What is left of women's dignity in the West?" he asked. He then came up with a statistic to drive home his point: "In Europe almost 70% of housewives are beaten by their husbands."

That was a self-serving lie. Western women, with few exceptions, are safe and free. Iranian women are neither. Officials like Attorney General Holder, the deputy constable of Gwent, and the activists and journalists who promoted the Super Bowl and World Cup hoaxes, unwittingly contribute to such twisted deceptions.

Victims of intimate violence are best served by the truth. Eric Holder should correct his department's website immediately.

The Rape Epidemic Is a Fiction

Kevin D. Williamson

Kevin D. Williamson is director of the William F. Buckley Jr. Fellowship in Political Journalism at the National Review Institute.

Rape is a vicious crime, one that disproportionately affects poor women and incarcerated men, but Barack Obama knows his voters, and so his recent remarks on the subject were focused not on penitentiaries, broken families, or Indian reservations but on college campuses, where the despicable crime is bound up in a broader feminist Kulturkampf only tangentially related to the very real problem of sexual violence against women.

The subject is a maddening one. President Obama repeated the endlessly reiterated but thoroughly debunked claim that one in five women will be sexually assaulted in her college years. The actual rate is . . . sort of an interesting problem, the information being so inconsistent and contradictory that one almost suspects that it is so by design.

President Obama, who gives every indication of being committed to the bitter end to his belief in the omnipotence of his merest utterance, gave a speech in which he affirmed his position that rape is wicked and that we should discourage it. Instead of giving a content-free speech, he should have directed his Department of Justice to put together some definitive data on the question.

Much of the scholarly literature estimates that the actual rate is more like a tenth of that one-in-five rate, 2.16 percent, or 21.6 per 1,000 to use the conventional formulation. But

Kevin D. Williamson, "The Rape Epidemic Is a Fiction," *National Review*, September 21, 2014. Copyright © 2014 National Review. All rights reserved. Reproduced with permission.

that number is problematic, too, as are most of the numbers related to sexual assault, as the National Institute of Justice, the DoJ's research arm, documents. For example, two surveys conducted practically in tandem produced victimization rates of 0.16 percent and 1.7 percent, respectively—i.e., the latter estimate was *eleven times* the former. The NIJ blames defective wording on survey questions.

It is probably the case that the prevalence of sexual assault on college campuses is wildly exaggerated.

This is a matter of concern because a comparison between the NIJ's estimates of college-campus rape and the estimates of rape in the general population compiled by the DoJ's National Crime Victimization Survey implies that the rate of rape among college students is more than ten times that of the general population.

It is not impossible that this is the case, but there is significant cause for skepticism. For example, in the general population college-age women have significantly lower rates of sexual assault than do girls twelve to seventeen, while a fifth of all rape victims are younger than twelve. Most of the familiar demographic trends in violent crime are reflected in the rape statistics: Poor women are sexually assaulted at twice the rate of women in households earning $50,000 a year or more; African American women are victimized at higher rates than are white women, while Native American women are assaulted at twice the rate of white women; divorced and never-married women are assaulted at seven times the rate of married women; women in urban communities are assaulted at higher rates than those in the suburbs, and those in rural areas are assaulted at dramatically higher rates. But there is at least one significant departure from the usual trends in violent crime: Only about 9 percent of those raped are men.

It is probably the case that the prevalence of sexual assault on college campuses is wildly exaggerated—not necessarily in absolute terms, but relative to the rate of sexual assault among college-aged women with similar demographic characteristics who are not attending institutions of higher learning. The DoJ hints at this in its criticism of survey questions, some of which define "sexual assault" so loosely as to include actions that "are not criminal." This might explain why so many women who answer survey questions in a way consistent with their being counted victims of sexual assault frequently display such a blasé attitude toward the events in question and so rarely report them. As the DoJ study puts it: "The most commonly reported response—offered by more than half the students— was that they did not think the incident was serious enough to report. More than 35 percent said they did not report the incident because they were unclear as to whether a crime was committed or that harm was intended."

If you are having a little trouble getting your head around a definition of "sexual assault" so liberal that it includes everything from forcible rape at gunpoint to acts that not only fail to constitute crimes under the law but leave the victims "unclear as to whether harm was intended," then you are, unlike much of our culture, still sane.

The way we talk about rape suggests that we do not much care about the facts of the case.

Of all the statistics and evidence that are prevalent in the discussion of sexual assault, there is one datum conspicuous in its absence: the fact that sexual assault has been cut by nearly two-thirds since 1995. Under the Bureau of Justice Statistics' apples-to-apples year-over-year comparison, sexual assault has declined 64 percent since the Clinton years. That is excellent news, indeed, but it does not feed the rape-epidemic narrative, and so it must be set aside.

The fictitious rape epidemic is necessary to support the fiction of "rape culture," by which feminists mean anything other than an actual rape culture, for example the culture of the Pakistani immigrant community in Rotherham in the United Kingdom. "Rape culture" simply means speech or thought that feminists disapprove of and wish to suppress, and the concept has been deployed in the cause of, inter alia, bringing disciplinary action against a Harvard student who wrote a satire of feminist rhetoric, forbidding politically unpopular speakers from speaking on campuses, and encouraging what often has turned out to be headlong and grotesquely unjust rushes to judgment, as in the case of the Duke lacrosse team. Feminism is about political power, and not the Susan B. Anthony ("positively voted the Republican ticket—straight") full-citizenship model of political power but rather one dominated by a very small band of narrow ideologues still operating under the daft influence of such theorists as Andrea Dworkin and Catharine MacKinnon, each of whom in her way equated political opposition to feminism with rape.

This has some worrisome practical results, not the least of which is muddying the water on the issue of sexual assault itself. For example, feminists energetically protest that advising women to take such precautionary measures as moderating their alcohol intake at college parties is a species of rape-culture victim-blaming (rather than reasonable advice), and so it is no surprise that, as the DoJ notes, many surveys inquire of rape victims whether they believed their attackers to have been under the influence of drugs or alcohol but decline to ask the victims whether they were under the influence. Evidence very strongly suggests that rapists frequently use intoxicants, openly or surreptitiously, as part of a strategy conceived with malice aforethought to render their victims vulnerable. It might be useful to know how often this is the case and how often it works or fails to work, but we will not know if we refuse to ask the question.

Our policy debates are dominated by relatively narrow-minded and self-interested elites, and so it is natural that our discussion of sexual assault focuses on what might be happening at Villanova University rather than what's happening on Riker's Island or on Ojibwe reservations. But the way we talk about rape suggests that we do not much care about the facts of the case. If understanding and preventing rape were our motive, we'd know whether the victimization rate was x or $11x$, and whether elite college campuses are in *fact* rather than in rhetoric more dangerous than crime-ridden ghettos and isolated villages in Alaska, a state in which the rate of rape is three times the national average. We'd never accept that the National Bureau of Economic Research didn't know whether the inflation rate were 1.6 percent or 17 percent. We'd give the issue properly rigorous consideration.

But if your interest were in making opposition to feminist political priorities a quasi-criminal offense and using the horrific crime of rape as a cultural and political cudgel, then you'd be doing about what we're doing right now.

There Is No So-Called Rape Culture

Cathy Young

Cathy Young writes a weekly column for the news website Real-ClearPolitics and is also a contributing editor at Reason *magazine.*

December [2014] has not been a good month for the feminist crusade against the "rape culture."

A Rape Hoax

The *Rolling Stone* account of a horrific fraternity gang rape at the University of Virginia [UVA], which many advocates saw as a possible "tipping point"—a shocking wake-up call demonstrating that even the most brutal sexual assaults on our college campuses are tacitly tolerated—has unraveled to the point where only a true believer would object to calling it a rape hoax.

At first, when investigative reporting by *The Washington Post* revealed major holes in the story, activists as well as feminist commentators chastised those who were too quick to declare it discredited. Just because *Rolling Stone* screwed up its reporting, they said, doesn't mean that Jackie was not sexually assaulted or that her complaint was not neglected by the university. Just because Jackie changed her story, they insisted, doesn't make her a liar—merely a likely rape victim whose trauma-fogged memory caused her to get some details wrong. (Her story, let's not forget, had changed from being forced to perform oral sex on five men to being vaginally raped by seven men, punched in the face, and cut on shattered glass.)

Cathy Young, "The Crusade Against 'Rape Culture' Stumbles," RealClearPolitics, December 23, 2014. Copyright © 2014 Real Clear Politics. All rights reserved. Reproduced with permission.

"The man that Jackie describes, named 'Drew' in the story, is a real person on campus," wrote leading feminist pundit Amanda Marcotte, referring to Jackie's date who supposedly brought her to a fraternity party and lured her into a rape trap. "He just happens to belong to another fraternity on campus. Which means that, while there's a chance she's lying, there's also a very big and very real chance that this all happened and she just forgot what frat house it was at."

Now, it turns out "Drew"—or "Haven Monahan," the name Jackie originally gave her friends—doesn't seem to exist after all, on the UVA campus, anywhere in the United States, or probably anywhere on the planet. His name is straight out of a particularly cheesy romance novel; his photo, which Jackie's friends got in text messages, turned out to match a former high school classmate of hers who goes to a different college. It also looks like Jackie made up both "Haven" and the sexual assault he supposedly engineered in an attempt to get the romantic attention of Ryan Duffin, one of the friends she called for help that night. Tellingly, her lawyer has not commented on these revelations. The only alternate explanation is that Jackie is the victim of a diabolically clever frame-up by her ex-friends.

The National Crime Victimization Survey (NCVS) ... found that approximately 6 out of 1,000 college women say they have been sexually assaulted in the past year. ... Still a troubling figure, to be sure, but it does not quite bear out claims that the American campus is a war-against-women zone.

Assuming Jackie is a fabulist, one can debate how much blame she deserves. It's clear she's a troubled young woman, and somewhat in her defense she did not falsely accuse any actual men (though it certainly seems that she falsely accused her former friends, two men and one woman, of treating her brutal rape as a minor unpleasantness far less important than invitations to frat parties). It is also clear that she was exploited by author Sabrina Rubin Erdely, and arguably *Rolling Stone* too, in pursuit of a sensational story. But some of the blame must go to the movement that encouraged her in turning her fantasy of victimhood into activism—especially when that movement is so entrenched in its true-believer mindset that some of its adherents seem unable to accept contrary facts. Katherine Ripley, executive editor of the UVA student newspaper, *The Cavalier Daily*, continued to post #IStandWithJackie tweets for days after the "Haven Monahan" story broke. Two other UVA students made a video thanking Jackie for "pulling back the curtain" on campus rape and praising her "bravery."

The Real Statistics of Sexual Assault

Meanwhile, even as the UVA saga unfolded, the "women's page" of the online magazine *Slate*, Double X, published an outstanding long article by liberal journalist Emily Yoffe examining the excesses of the campus rape crusade—from the use of shoddy statistics to hype an "epidemic" of sexual violence against college women to the rise of policies that trample the civil rights of accused male students. The piece was retweeted nearly 2,500 times and received a great deal of positive attention, partly no doubt on the wave of the UVA/*Rolling Stone* scandal. Some of Yoffe's critique echoes arguments made earlier by a number of mostly conservative and libertarian commentators. But, apart from the extensive and careful research she brings to the table, the fact that these arguments were given a platform in one of the premier feminist media spaces is something of a breakthrough, if not a turning point.

Just days after the publication of Yoffe's article, the Department of Justice [DOJ] Bureau of Justice Statistics [BJS] released a new study boosting her case (and based on data she briefly discussed). The special report, "Rape and Sexual Assault Victimization Among College-Age Females, 1995–2013," shows that not only are female college students less likely to experience sexual assault than non-college women 18 to 24, but the rate at which they are sexually assaulted is nowhere near the "one in five" or "one in four" statistics brandished by advocates. The National Crime Victimization Survey (NCVS), from which the BJS derives its data, found that approximately 6 out of 1,000 college women say they have been sexually assaulted in the past year. Over four years of college, economist Mark Perry points out, this adds up to about one in 53. Still a troubling figure, to be sure, but it does not quite bear out claims that the American campus is a war-against-women zone.

While the stories told by students are often compelling, it is important to remember that they are personal narratives which may or may not be factual.

Journalists who embrace the narrative of campus anti-rape activism, such as *The Huffington Post*'s Tyler Kingkade and Vox.com's Libby Nelson, have tried to rebut claims that the new DOJ report discredits the higher advocacy numbers. Kingkade asserts that the NCVS "doesn't look at incapacitated rape," in which the perpetrator takes advantage of the victim's severe intoxication or unconsciousness. Nelson argues that because the survey focuses on crime victimization, respondents may underreport acquaintance rapes which don't fit the stereotype of the stranger with a knife jumping out of the bushes.

But neither criticism holds up. The standard question used in the NCVS to screen for sexual victimization is, "Have you been forced or coerced to engage in unwanted sexual activity by (a) someone you didn't know before, (b) a casual acquaintance? OR (c) someone you know well?" In other words, respondents are explicitly encouraged to report non-stranger sexual assaults—and, while they are not specifically asked about being assaulted while incapacitated, the wording certainly does not exclude such attacks.

Time for a Reassessment

Kingkade also suggests that the numbers are beside the point, since the effort to combat campus sexual assault is about people, not statistics—specifically, "about students who said they were wronged by their schools after they were raped." Of course every rape is a tragedy, on campus or off—all the more if the victim finds no redress. But if it happens to one in five women during their college years, this is not just a tragedy but a crisis that arguably justifies emergency measures—which is why proponents of sweeping new policies have repeatedly invoked these scary numbers. (Sen. Kristen Gillibrand, Democrat of New York, has now had the one-in-five figure removed from her website.) And while the stories told by students are often compelling, it is important to remember that they are personal narratives which may or may not be factual. Only last June, Emily Renda, a UVA graduate and activist who now works at the school, included Jackie's story—under the pseudonym "Jenna"—in her testimony before a Senate committee.

Of course this is not to suggest that most such accounts are fabricated; but they are also filtered through subjective experience, memory, and personal bias. Yet, for at least three years, these stories have been accorded virtually uncritical reception by the mainstream media. When I had a chance to investigate one widely publicized college case—that of Brown University students Lena Sclove and Daniel Kopin—for a feature in *The Daily Beast*, the facts turned out to bear little resemblance to the media narrative of a brutal rape punished with a slap on the wrist.

Now, in what may be another sign of turning tides, the accused in another high-profile case is getting his say. *The New York Times* has previously given ample coverage to Emma Sulkowicz, the Columbia University student famous for carrying around a mattress to protest the school's failure to expel her alleged rapist. Now, it has allowed that man, Paul Nungesser, to tell his story—a story of being ostracized and targeted by mob justice despite being cleared of all charges in a system far less favorable to the accused than criminal courts. No one knows whether Sulkowicz or Nungesser is telling the truth; but the media have at last acknowledged that there is another side to this story.

Will 2015 see a pushback against the anti-"rape culture" movement on campus? If so, good. This is a movement that has capitalized on laudable sympathy for victims of sexual assault to promote gender warfare, misinformation and moral panic. It's time for a reassessment.

CHAPTER 2

What Causes Violence Against Women?

Chapter Preface

There is much debate about what causes violence against women. Is violence perpetrated by men against women a product of culture? Are men prone to violence due to their physiology? Does violence against women result from both cultural and biological causes? Answering these questions matters, since although there may be much debate about the causes of violence against women, there is virtually no debate about whether it should be stopped. Yet, figuring out the best approaches to ending violence against women depends upon answering these questions about its causes. One debate about the cause of rape illuminates the challenges and questions that arise when attempting to explain what is behind men's sexual violence against women.

Feminist author Susan Brownmiller wrote in 1975—in her highly controversial book, *Against Our Will*—that men use rape as a tool of intimidation against women:

> Man's discovery that his genitalia could serve as a weapon to generate fear must rank as one of the most important discoveries of prehistoric times, along with the use of fire and the first crude stone axe. From prehistoric times to the present, I believe, rape has played a critical function. It is nothing more or less than a conscious process of intimidation by which all men keep all women in a state of fear.[1]

Brownmiller sees sexual violence as less about sex and more about "man's basic weapon of force against woman, the principal agent of his will and her fear." She argues, "Rape is a crime not of lust, but of violence and power."[2] Her view was revolutionary at the time, given that it explained sexual vio-

---

1. Susan Brownmiller, "The Mass Psychology of Rape: An Introduction," in *Against Our Will*, New York: Simon and Schuster, 1975, pp. 11–15.

2. Ibid.

lence in terms of power and dominance, rather than uncontrollable lust. In that sense, there was nothing a woman could do to prevent rape.

Evolutionary biologist Randy Thornhill and evolutionary anthropologist Craig T. Palmer challenged Brownmiller's view in their 2000 article, "Why Men Rape," published in the *New York Academy of Sciences* journal. They argue that the various facts about rape "make sense when rape is viewed as a natural, biological phenomenon that is a product of the human evolutionary heritage."[3] They see rape as one kind of sexual strategy that men developed with the goal of reproduction. They caution that by claiming that rape is natural, they do not intend to claim that it is justified, thereby committing a naturalistic fallacy. Nonetheless, Thornhill and Palmer do claim that since rape is about sex and is driven by sexual desire, "women should also be advised that the way they dress can put them at risk."[4]

Author Barbara Ehrenreich raised some objections to the evolutionary account of rape in her article "How 'Natural' Is Rape?," published in *Time*. She claims that the theory proposed by Thornhill and Palmer runs counter to the tenets of evolutionary psychology itself—namely that there is evolutionary value to parenting, something rapists do not provide. Furthermore, Ehrenreich argues that the level of violence present in rape and the amount of damage rape causes to women undermines an evolutionary account from a Darwinian perspective: "It's a pretty dumb Darwinian specimen who can't plant his seed without breaking the 'vessel' in the process," she writes. Ehrenreich also questions the conclusion that since men are prone to rape out of sexual desire, women ought to be careful about how they dress; she responds, "But

3. Randy Thornhill and Craig T. Palmer, "Why Men Rape," *New York Academy of Sciences*, January/February 2000. http://iranscope.ghandchi.com/Anthology/Women/rape.htm.

4. Ibid.

where is the evidence that women in mini-skirts are more likely to be raped than women in dirndls? Women were raped by the thousands in Bosnia, for example, and few if any of them were wearing bikinis or bustiers."[5]

As this debate shows, even the question of whether or not rape is about sex or violence is rife with disagreement. Thornhill and Palmer illustrate what is at stake: if rape is about sexual desire, then preventing rape may involve women doing anything possible to minimize the sexual desire of men. Yet, if rape is primarily about violence, it does not matter if women are sexually attractive to men. As the authors in this chapter illustrate, the debate about the possible causes of violence against women is informed by myriad, often opposing, views—on everything from the nature of violence to the culture of masculinity to the steps women can take to reduce that violence.

5. Barbara Ehrenreich, "How 'Natural' Is Rape?," *Time*, January 23, 2000. http://content.time.com/time/magazine/article/0,9171,38013,00.html.

Tyrannical Military Culture Causes Violence Against Women

Ann Jones

Ann Jones is author of They Were Soldiers: How the Wounded Return from America's Wars—The Untold Story.

Picture this. A man, armored in tattoos, bursts into a living room not his own. He confronts an enemy. He barks orders. He throws that enemy into a chair. Then against a wall. He plants himself in the middle of the room, feet widespread, fists clenched, muscles straining, face contorted in a scream of rage. The tendons in his neck are taut with the intensity of his terrifying performance. He chases the enemy to the next room, stopping escape with a quick grab and thrust and body block that pins the enemy, bent back, against a counter. He shouts more orders: his enemy can go with him to the basement for a "private talk," or be beaten to a pulp right here. Then he wraps his fingers around the neck of his enemy and begins to choke her.

A Militarized Culture

No, that invader isn't an American soldier leading a night raid on an Afghan village, nor is the enemy an anonymous Afghan householder. This combat warrior is just a guy in Ohio named Shane. He's doing what so many men find exhilarating: disciplining his girlfriend with a heavy dose of the violence we render harmless by calling it "domestic."

It's easy to figure out from a few basic facts that Shane is a skilled predator. Why else does a 31-year-old man lavish at-

Ann Jones, "Men Who Kick Down Doors: Tyrants at Home and Abroad," TomDispatch .com, March 21, 2013. Copyright © 2013 TomDispatch.com. All rights reserved. Reproduced with permission.

tention on a pretty 19-year-old with two children (ages four and two, the latter an equally pretty and potentially targeted little female)? And what more vulnerable girlfriend could he find than this one, named Maggie: a neglected young woman, still a teenager, who for two years had been raising her kids on her own while her husband fought a war in Afghanistan? That war had broken the family apart, leaving Maggie with no financial support and more alone than ever.

Official America, as embodied in our political system and national security state, now seems to be thoroughly masculine, paranoid, quarrelsome, secretive, greedy, aggressive, and violent.

But the way Shane assaulted Maggie, he might just as well have been a night-raiding soldier terrorizing an Afghan civilian family in pursuit of some dangerous Talib, real or imagined. For all we know, Maggie's estranged husband/soldier might have acted in the same way in some Afghan living room and not only been paid but also honored for it. The basic behavior is quite alike: an overwhelming display of superior force. The tactics: shock and awe. The goal: to control the behavior, the very life, of the designated target. The mind set: a sense of entitlement when it comes to determining the fate of a subhuman creature. The dark side: the fear and brutal rage of a scared loser who inflicts his miserable self on others.

As for that designated enemy, just as American exceptionalism asserts the superiority of the United States over all other countries and cultures on Earth, and even over the laws that govern international relations, misogyny—which seems to inform so much in the United States these days, from military boot camp to the Oscars to full frontal political assaults on a woman's right to control her own body—assures even the most pathetic guys like Shane of their innate superiority over some "thing" usually addressed with multiple obscenities.

Since 9/11, the further militarization of our already militarized culture has reached new levels. Official America, as embodied in our political system and national security state, now seems to be thoroughly masculine, paranoid, quarrelsome, secretive, greedy, aggressive, and violent. Readers familiar with "domestic violence" will recognize those traits as equally descriptive of the average American wife beater: scared but angry and aggressive, and feeling absolutely entitled to control something, whether it's just a woman, or a small wretched country like Afghanistan.

Connecting the Dots

It was John Stuart Mill, writing in the nineteenth century, who connected the dots between "domestic" and international violence. But he didn't use our absurdly gender-neutral, pale gray term "domestic violence." He called it "wife torture" or "atrocity," and he recognized that torture and atrocity are much the same, no matter where they take place—whether today in Guantanamo Bay, Cuba, Wardak Province, Afghanistan, or a bedroom or basement in Ohio. Arguing in 1869 against the subjection of women, Mill wrote that the Englishman's habit of household tyranny and "wife torture" established the pattern and practice for his foreign policy. The tyrant at home becomes the tyrant at war. Home is the training ground for the big games played overseas.

When tyranny and violence are practiced on a grand scale in foreign lands, the practice also intensifies at home.

Mill believed that, in early times, strong men had used force to enslave women and the majority of their fellow men. By the nineteenth century, however, the "law of the strongest" seemed to him to have been "abandoned"—in England at least—"as the regulating principle of the world's affairs." Slavery had been renounced. Only in the household did it continue to be practiced, though wives were no longer openly enslaved but merely "subjected" to their husbands. This subjection, Mill said, was the last vestige of the archaic "law of the strongest," and must inevitably fade away as reasonable men recognized its barbarity and injustice. Of his own time, he wrote that "nobody professes" the law of the strongest, and "as regards most of the relations between human beings, nobody is permitted to practice it."

Well, even a feminist may not be right about everything. Times often change for the worse, and rarely has the law of the strongest been more popular than it is in the United States today. Routinely now we hear congressmen declare that the U.S. is the greatest nation in the world because it is the greatest military power in history, just as presidents now regularly insist that the U.S. military is "the finest fighting force in the history of the world." Never mind that it rarely wins a war. Few here question that primitive standard—the law of the strongest—as the measure of this America's dwindling "civilization."

The War Against Women

Mill, however, was right about the larger point: that tyranny at home is the model for tyranny abroad. What he perhaps didn't see was the perfect reciprocity of the relationship that perpetuates the law of the strongest both in the home and far away.

When tyranny and violence are practiced on a grand scale in foreign lands, the practice also intensifies at home. As American militarism went into overdrive after 9/11, it validated violence against women here, where Republicans held up reauthorization of the Violence Against Women Act (first passed in 1994), and celebrities who publicly assaulted their girlfriends faced no consequences other than a deluge of sympathetic girl-fan tweets.

America's invasions abroad also validated violence within the U.S. military itself. An estimated 19,000 women soldiers were sexually assaulted in 2011; and an unknown number have been murdered by fellow soldiers who were, in many cases, their husbands or boyfriends. A great deal of violence against women in the military, from rape to murder, has been documented, only to be casually covered up by the chain of command.

Violence against civilian women here at home, on the other hand, may not be reported or tallied at all, so the full extent of it escapes notice. Men prefer to maintain the historical fiction that violence in the home is a private matter, properly and legally concealed behind a "curtain." In this way is male impunity and tyranny maintained.

Women cling to a fiction of our own: that we are much more "equal" than we are. Instead of confronting male violence, we still prefer to lay the blame for it on individual women and girls who fall victim to it—as if they had volunteered. But then, how to explain the dissonant fact that at least one of every three female American soldiers is sexually assaulted by a male "superior"? Surely that's not what American women had in mind when they signed up for the Marines or for Air Force flight training. In fact, lots of teenage girls volunteer for the military precisely to escape violence and sexual abuse in their childhood homes or streets.

Like the combat soldier in a foreign war who is modeled after him, [Shane] uses violence to hold his life together and accomplish his mission.

Don't get me wrong, military men are neither alone nor out of the ordinary in terrorizing women. The broader American war against women has intensified on many fronts here at home, right along with our wars abroad. Those foreign wars have killed uncounted thousands of civilians, many of them women and children, which could make the private battles of domestic warriors like Shane here in the U.S. seem puny by comparison. But it would be a mistake to underestimate the firepower of the Shanes of our American world. The statistics tell us that a legal handgun has been the most popular means of dispatching a wife, but when it comes to girlfriends, guys really get off on beating them to death.

Some 3,073 people were killed in the terrorist attacks on the United States on 9/11. Between that day and June 6, 2012, 6,488 U.S. soldiers were killed in combat in Iraq and Afghanistan, bringing the death toll for America's war on terror at home and abroad to 9,561. During the same period, 11,766 women were murdered in the United States by their husbands or boyfriends, both military and civilian. The greater number of women killed here at home is a measure of the scope and the furious intensity of the war against women, a war that threatens to continue long after the misconceived war on terror is history.

The Documentation of Abuse

Think about Shane, standing there in a nondescript living room in Ohio screaming his head off like a little child who wants what he wants when he wants it. Reportedly, he was trying to be a good guy and make a career as a singer in a Christian rock band. But like the combat soldier in a foreign war who is modeled after him, he uses violence to hold his life together and accomplish his mission.

We know about Shane only because there happened to be a photographer on the scene. Sara Naomi Lewkowicz had chosen to document the story of Shane and his girlfriend Maggie out of sympathy for his situation as an ex-con, recently released from prison yet not free of the stigma attached to a man who had done time. Then, one night, there he was in the living room throwing Maggie around, and Lewkowicz did what any good combat photographer would do as a witness to history: she kept shooting. That action alone was a kind of intervention and may have saved Maggie's life.

In the midst of the violence, Lewkowicz also dared to snatch from Shane's pocket her own cell phone, which he had borrowed earlier. It's unclear whether she passed the phone to someone else or made the 911 call herself. The police arrested Shane, and a smart policewoman told Maggie: "You know, he's not going to stop. They never stop. They usually stop when they kill you."

Maggie did the right thing. She gave the police a statement. Shane is back in prison. And Lewkowicz's remarkable photographs were posted online on February 27th at *Time* magazine's website feature *Lightbox* under the heading "Photographer As Witness: A Portrait of Domestic Violence."

The photos are remarkable because the photographer is very good and the subject of her attention is so rarely caught on camera. Unlike warfare covered in Iraq and Afghanistan by embedded combat photographers, wife torture takes place mostly behind closed doors, unannounced and unrecorded. The first photographs of wife torture to appear in the U.S. were Donna Ferrato's now iconic images of violence against women at home.

Like Lewkowicz, Ferrato came upon wife torture by chance; she was documenting a marriage in 1980 when the happy husband chose to beat up his wife. Yet so reluctant were photo editors to pull aside the curtain of domestic privacy that even after Ferrato became a *Life* photographer in 1984, pursuing the same subject, nobody, including *Life*, wanted to publish the shocking images she produced.

Reaction to the Photographs

In 1986, six years after she witnessed that first assault, some of her photographs of violence against women in the home were published in the *Philadelphia Inquirer*, and brought her the 1987 Robert F. Kennedy journalism award "for outstanding coverage of the problems of the disadvantaged." In 1991, Aperture, the publisher of distinguished photography books, brought out Ferrato's eye-opening body of work as *Living with the Enemy* (for which I wrote an introduction). Since then, the photos have been widely reproduced. *Time* used a Ferrato image on its cover in 1994, when the murder of Nicole Brown Simpson briefly drew attention to what the magazine called "the epidemic of domestic abuse" and *Lightbox* featured a small retrospective of her domestic violence work on June 27, 2012.

Ferrato herself started a foundation, offering her work to women's groups across the country to exhibit at fundraisers for local shelters and services. Those photo exhibitions also helped raise consciousness across America and certainly contributed to smarter, less misogynistic police procedures of the kind that put Shane back in jail.

So many find it convenient to ignore the violence that America's warriors abroad inflict under orders on a mass scale upon women and children in war zones.

Ferrato's photos were incontrovertible evidence of the violence in our homes, rarely acknowledged and never before so plainly seen. Yet until February 27th, when with Ferrato's help, Sara Naomi Lewkowicz's photos were posted on *Lightbox* only two months after they were taken, Ferrato's photos were all we had. We needed more. So there was every reason for Lewkowicz's work to be greeted with acclaim by photographers and women everywhere.

Instead, in more than 1,700 comments posted at *Lightbox*, photographer Lewkowicz was mainly castigated for things like not dropping her camera and taking care to get Maggie's distraught two-year-old daughter out of the room or singlehandedly stopping the assault. (Need it be said that stopping combat is not the job of combat photographers?)

Maggie, the victim of this felonious assault, was also mercilessly denounced: for going out with Shane in the first place, for failing to foresee his violence, for "cheating" on her already estranged husband fighting in Afghanistan, and inexplicably for being a "perpetrator." Reviewing the commentary for the *Columbia Journalism Review*, Jina Moore concluded, "[T]here's one thing all the critics seem to agree on: The only adult in the house *not* responsible for the violence is the man committing it."

The War Abroad and at Home

Viewers of these photographs—photos that accurately reflect the daily violence so many women face—seem to find it easy to ignore, or even to praise, the raging man behind it all. So, too, do so many find it convenient to ignore the violence that America's warriors abroad inflict under orders on a mass scale upon women and children in war zones.

The U.S. invasion and occupation of Iraq had the effect of displacing millions from their homes within the country or driving them into exile in foreign lands. Rates of rape and atrocity were staggering, as I learned firsthand when in 2008–2009 I spent time in Syria, Jordan, and Lebanon talking with Iraqi refugees. In addition, those women who remain in Iraq now live under the rule of conservative Islamists, heavily influenced by Iran. Under the former secular regime, Iraqi women were considered the most advanced in the Arab world; today, they say they have been set back a century.

In Afghanistan, too, while Americans take credit for putting women back in the workplace and girls in school, untold thousands of women and children have been displaced internally, many to makeshift camps on the outskirts of Kabul where 17 children froze to death last January [2013]. The U.N. reported 2,754 civilian deaths and 4,805 civilian injuries as a result of the war in 2012, the majority of them women and children. In a country without a state capable of counting bodies, these are undoubtedly significant undercounts. A U.N. official said, "It is the tragic reality that most Afghan women and girls were killed or injured while engaging in their everyday activities." Thousands of women in Afghan cities have been forced into survival sex, as were Iraqi women who fled as refugees to Beirut and Damascus.

That's what male violence is meant to do to women. The enemy. War itself is a kind of screaming tattooed man, standing in the middle of a room—or another country—asserting the law of the strongest. It's like a reset button on history that almost invariably ensures women will find themselves subjected to men in ever more terrible ways. It's one more thing that, to a certain kind of man, makes going to war, like good old-fashioned wife torture, so exciting and so much fun.

Our Military, Ourselves: Why Americans Are to Blame for the Pentagon's Outrageous Sex Scandals

Micah Zenko and Amelia Mae Wolf

Micah Zenko is the Douglas Dillon Fellow and Amelia Mae Wolf a research associate with the Center for Preventive Action at the Council on Foreign Relations.

Ongoing rampant sexual assault within America's armed forces is a tragedy. The 2012 Workplace and Gender Relations Survey of Active Duty Members (WGRA) found that an estimated 26,000 active-duty servicemembers were sexually assaulted last year, and recent allegations of sexual assault by officers assigned to prevent that very crime have lent the situation a sinister irony. The U.S. military is clearly facing, in the words of Chairman of the Joint Chiefs of Staff Gen. Martin Dempsey, "a crisis."

Last week, Gen. Mark Welsh, the Air Force chief of staff, declared that confronting the problem was his "No. 1 priority." Army Chief of Staff Gen. Ray Odierno went further, saying: "The Army is failing in its efforts to combat sexual assault and sexual harassment." He said that fighting the crime is now "our primary mission." Repeating the claims of his two predecessors, Defense Secretary Chuck Hagel vowed to solve the chronic problem of sexual assault and stated that "every option is on the table."

The estimated incidents of "unwanted sexual contact" within the military have increased since the previous survey in

Micah Zenko and Amelia Mae Wolf, "Our Military, Ourselves: Why Americans Are to Blame for the Pentagon's Outrageous Sex Scandals," *Foreign Policy*, May 22, 2013. Copyright © 2013 Foreign Policy. All rights reserved. Reproduced with permission.

2010 despite internal reforms. When reviewing the Pentagon and service websites dedicated to preventing sexual assault, it is difficult to comprehend the vast number of new directives, memoranda, instructions, policies, and awareness-raising campaigns that have been introduced over the past three years— none of which seems to be having an effect. Nancy Parrish, president of Protect Our Defenders, referred to these efforts as "half-hearted, half-measured reform Band-Aids."

The prevalence of sexual assault within the ranks [of the military] is a snapshot of the crisis facing the United States.

Unfortunately, however admirable the recent condemnations of sexual assault in the military, they're unlikely to have much impact, because sexual assault in the military is not a military problem. It is an *American* problem. Scholars, retired officers, and others have longed warned of the creeping militarization of American society. However, as the Pentagon yet again renews its sexual assault prevention efforts, it must not discount the socialization of the American military.

The data suggest that one servicemember is sexually assaulted every 20 minutes and that one American citizen is sexually assaulted every two minutes, but it is difficult to directly compare military and civilian sexual assault rates. The WGRA defines "unwanted sexual contact" as "completed or attempted sexual intercourse, sodomy (oral or anal sex), penetration by an object, and the unwanted touching of genitalia and other sexually-related areas of the body." Survey participants were asked to report incidents occurring in the past 12 months. Meanwhile, the Department of Justice survey used to calculate sexual assaults nationwide asks participants if anyone has "attacked" or "threatened" them by "grabbing, punching, or choking" or by "any rape, attempted rape or other type of sexual act" over the course of the past six months.

According to the Centers for Disease Control and Prevention's most recent survey on the nationwide prevalence of sexual violence, 5.3 percent of English- and/or Spanish-speaking American women age 18 and older, who were not institutionalized or in the armed forces, were victims of unwanted sexual contact, including rape and other acts of sexual violence, in 2010. An estimated 4.9 percent of men experienced forms of sexual violence other than rape. (Unfortunately, the sample population of males reported too few incidents of rape for an estimate to be determined, which may allude to a low reporting rate rather than a low incident rate.)

Although sexual violence has decreased nationwide over the past two decades, that downward trend cannot be taken for granted because we do not know why it happened. And, regardless, the number of incidents remains shockingly high. Within the military, 6.1 percent of female servicemembers and 1.2 percent of male servicemembers reported unwanted sexual contact in 2012. The prevalence of sexual assault within the ranks is a snapshot of the crisis facing the United States, where "13% of women and 6% of men are sexually coerced in their lifetimes," according to the CDC.

Despite progress in many areas, American culture remains bluntly sexist—and has become increasingly sexualized.

Military officials' attempts to blame the crisis on American society have understandably been clumsy. During a May 7 Senate Armed Services Committee hearing, Gen. Welsh attributed the rates of sexual assault in the military, in part, to the "hookup mentality of junior high." He later apologized for the remark, noting that he wished he had taken more time to explain himself. He added: "We have to get at instilling from the day people walk in the door in our Air Force this idea of respect, inclusion, diversity, and value of every individual."

But Welsh had a good point: No one who enters the military does so with a blank slate. All servicemembers have at least 17 years of cultural experience prior to signing up. One need only flip through a few channels on cable television or spend a few moments surfing the Internet to understand, as Tom Vanden Brook and Gregg Zoroya noted in a recent article, that male servicemembers (who make up 85 percent of the military) are drawn from a society in which "violence and objectification of women are staple elements."

American women are born into a society in which the "importance" of beauty and sexuality is emphasized in their personal and professional lives. Despite great achievements in gender equality, sexism persists in the United States and frequently goes unnoticed because it is so deeply engrained in our culture. "It seems to be increasingly difficult to talk about sexism, equality and women's rights in a modern society that perceives itself to have achieved gender equality," writes Laura Bates, founder of the Everyday Sexism Project, which uses social media to measure sexism faced by women. In truth, the United States remains far from gender equality: last year, it was ranked 42nd on the Gender Inequality Index, which quantifies and analyzes reproductive health, political and educational empowerment, and participation in the labor force.

Despite progress in many areas, American culture remains bluntly sexist—and has become increasingly sexualized. The Disney princess movies, which are still a childhood staple of most American girls, convey that beauty and sexuality are key to "happily ever after." The music industry is no different. A 2012 study by Cynthia Frisby and Jennifer Aubrey found that female artists are increasingly using sexual imagery to brand their products and that "young audiences may interpret these sexually objectifying images as important ways to be seen as attractive and valuable to society." Natasha Walter, author of *Living Dolls*, wrote that, as a result, women are confusing sexual objectification with empowerment. Of course, men also face daunting social expectations to be powerful, strong, and "manly."

Sexism is also evident in more glaring forms. Just this past weekend, radio host Pete Santilli casually remarked that Hillary Clinton should be "shot in the vagina"—vulgar, gender-based language that belittled and threatened the former secretary of state. In a similar instance just over a year ago, Rush Limbaugh proudly referred to Sandra Fluke, a law student at Georgetown University, as a "slut" and a "prostitute" because she believed that health insurance companies should cover the cost of contraceptives.

Addressing [the] sexual assault crisis as solely a military problem would merely place another Band-Aid on a national wound.

Current and retired military officers should openly and repeatedly condemn sexism and the attendant pervasiveness of sexual assaults within society, just as they often warn about societal trends that negatively impact the ability to recruit, train, and equip the force. That's what they did with high school graduation rates and obesity—see the 2012 "Too Fat to Fight" study. If a lack of education or fitness can be categorized as threats to our national security, then surely sexual violence should qualify as well.

Last week, Pentagon Press Secretary George Little stated: "It is, in my opinion, and I believe the secretary's position, not good enough to compare us to the rest of society. This is the United States military and the Department of Defense. It really doesn't matter if our rates are similar to the rest of society, quite frankly. We must hold ourselves to a higher standard and that's what the American people demand." That may be so, but how can the issue be effectively addressed without improving standards throughout society?

If you spend any time at a post or base—much less a reserve depot or National Guard armory—you realize that the military is neither isolated nor insulated from American society, nor should it be. Addressing this sexual assault crisis as solely a military problem would merely place another Band-Aid on a national wound; success will elude even the most comprehensive military reforms. If policymakers and military officials wish to stand by their commitments to eradicate the culture of sexual violence in the military, they must confront its root cause.

On Friday, Hagel proclaimed: "We all have committed to turn this around, and we're going to fix the problem. . . . The problem will be solved here in this institution." No, Mr. Secretary, it won't.

One Way to End Violence Against Women? Married Dads

W. Bradford Wilcox and Robin Fretwell Wilson

W. Bradford Wilcox is a professor of sociology at the University of Virginia and Robin Fretwell Wilson is the Roger and Stephany Joslin Professor of Law and director of the program in family law and policy at the University of Illinois.

The dramatic social media response to the UC-Santa Barbara shooting, captured by the hashtag #YesAllWomen, underlined an important and unpleasant truth: across the United States, millions of girls and women have been abused, assaulted, or raped by men, and even more females fear that they will be subject to such an attack. As Sarah Kliff wrote in *Vox*: a "national survey of American women found that a slight majority (51.9 percent) reported experiencing physical violence at some point in their life."

The Risk of Violence

This social media outpouring makes it clear that *some men* pose a real threat to the physical and psychic welfare of women and girls. But obscured in the public conversation about the violence against women is the fact that *some other men* are more likely to protect women, directly and indirectly, from the threat of male violence: married biological fathers. The bottom line is this: Married women are notably safer than their unmarried peers, and girls raised in a home with their married father are markedly less likely to be abused or assaulted than children living without their own father.

W. Bradford Wilcox and Robin Fretwell Wilson, "One Way to End Violence Against Women? Married Dads," *Washington Post*, June 10, 2014. Copyright © 2014 Washington Post. All rights reserved. Reproduced with permission.

Start with the threat that girls face from men. One of the most comprehensive portraits of sexual and physical abuse of girls (and boys) comes from the Fourth National Incidence Study of Child Abuse and Neglect. As the figure above indicates, children are more likely to be abused when they do not live in a home with their married father. What's more: girls and boys are significantly more likely to be abused when they are living in a cohabiting household with an unrelated adult— usually their mother's boyfriend. Indeed, the report notes that "only 0.7 per 1,000 children living with two married biological parents were sexually abused, compared to 12.1 per 1,000 children living with a single parent who had an unmarried partner." The results from this federal study are consistent with academic research that indicates that "girls who are victimized are . . . more likely to have lived without their natural fathers," and that the risk is especially high when a boyfriend or stepfather is in the picture.

The "emotional support and the supervision" that engaged fathers provide to their children can limit their vulnerability to potential predators.

The risk of physical abuse also increases when a child lives without her father, once again, particularly when an unrelated boyfriend is in the home. A 2005 study published in *Pediatrics* found that "[c]hildren residing in households with unrelated adults were nearly 50 times as likely to die of inflicted injuries than children residing with 2 biological parents."

Women are also safer in married homes. As the figure above (derived from a recent Department of Justice study) indicates, married women are the least likely to be victimized by an intimate partner. They are also less likely to be the victims of violent crime in general. Overall, another U.S. Department of Justice study found that never-married women are nearly four times more likely to be victims of violent crime, compared to married women. The bottom line is that married women are less likely to be raped, assaulted, or robbed than their unmarried peers.

The Safety of Marriage

What's going on here? Why are women safer when married and children safer when living with their married biological parents? For girls, the research tells us that marriage provides a measure of stability and commitment to the adults' relationship, that married biological fathers are more likely to be attentive and engaged with their children because they expect the relationship to be enduring. As a consequence, unrelated males are less likely to have sustained interaction with children of the family when dad has a day-in-day-out presence in the home. More generally, the "emotional support and the supervision" that engaged fathers provide to their children can limit their vulnerability to potential predators, as David Finkelhor, director of the University of New Hampshire Crimes Against Children Research Center, has observed.

For women, part of the story is about what social scientists call a "selection effect," namely, women in healthy, safe relationships are more likely to select into marriage, and women in unhealthy, unsafe relationships often lack the power to demand marriage or the desire to marry. Of course, women in high conflict marriages are more likely to select into divorce.

But marriage also seems to cause men to behave better. That's because men tend to settle down after they marry, to be more attentive to the expectations of friends and kin, to be more faithful, and to be more committed to their partners— factors that minimize the risk of violence. What's more: women who are married are more likely to live in safer neighborhoods, to have a partner who is watching out for their physical safety, and—for obvious reasons—to spend less time in settings that increase their risk of rape, robbery, and assaults.

To be sure, it doesn't take a viewing of *The Burning Bed* or *Safe Haven* to realize that married men can and do abuse or assault their wives or daughters. Marriage is no panacea when it comes to male violence. But married fathers are much less likely to resort to violence than men who are not tied by marriage or biology to a female. And, most fundamentally, for the girls and women in their lives, married fathers provide direct protection by watching out for the physical welfare of their wives and daughters, and indirect protection by increasing the odds they live in safe homes and are not exposed to men likely to pose a threat.

So, women: if you're the product of a good marriage, and feel safer as a consequence, lift a glass to dear old dad this Sunday.

Marriage Will Not Save Women from Male Violence

Amanda Marcotte

Amanda Marcotte is a DoubleX contributor at Slate.

The routine conservative exhortations to single women to hurry up and get married already became downright irresponsible on Tuesday [June 10, 2014] with W. Bradford Wilcox and Robin Fretwell Wilson's piece in the *Washington Post* titled "One way to end violence against women? Stop taking lovers and get married." It's not a well-argued essay (clearly) but kudos to Wilcox and Wilson for managing both to blame women for male violence and guilt-trip them for not marrying the first man they meet with a pulse. If only they had worked in a dig about cats.

Correlation, Not Causation

The headline is not misleading: The piece actually argues that marriage is the best prevention against violence for women. "The bottom line is this: Married women are notably safer than their unmarried peers, and girls raised in a home with their married father are markedly less likely to be abused or assaulted than children living without their own father," they write. Of course, while playing the game of manipulating statistics, they pointedly ignore the fact that *domestic violence rates have been falling* at *the same time marriage rates are falling*. I guess correlation only equals causation if it serves the right cause.

While Wilcox and Wilson tacitly admit that the correlation between marriage and lower rates of violence might be because "women in healthy, safe relationships are more likely to

Amanda Marcotte, "Marriage Will Not Save Women From Male Violence," *Slate*, June 10, 2014. Copyright © 2014 Slate. All rights reserved. Reproduced with permission.

select into marriage," most of the piece is an attempt to convince women that it's the presence of a wedding ring itself that reduces violence more than the likelier story, which is that abusive relationships often fall apart before the marriage begins.

The last thing that women in abusive relationships need is to be told that they can turn a bad man good by marrying him.

"But marriage also seems to cause men to behave better," Wilcox and Wilson write. "That's because men tend to settle down after they marry, to be more attentive to the expectations of friends and kin, to be more faithful, and to be more committed to their partners—factors that minimize the risk of violence." To sweeten the deal, they also promise that by squeezing that wedding ring onto his finger, you get to live in a better neighborhood and lower your chances of getting robbed. Taken as a whole, in fact, the piece reads like a threat: Get married or you face the violent consequences, ladies.

Look, there is no doubt that there's a correlation between being married and lower rates of violence, but it's not likely because marriage itself provides protection. It's because the same privileges that lead to higher rates of marriages—higher incomes, more education, older age—also lead to living in safer neighborhoods and having lower rates of interpersonal violence. Hijacking women's experiences of violence in order to bully them about being single isn't just tacky, but dishonest.

It's hard to overstate the gross negligence of this piece (which, by the way, is pegged to Father's Day). One of the most confounding issues when it comes to domestic violence is that many victims believe that if they just love a little harder and put a little more work into the relationship, they can turn an abusive partner into a loving one. Even though Wilcox and

Wilson admit "married men can and do abuse or assault their wives," they immediately return to arguing that "married fathers are much less likely to resort to violence," as if the marriage itself was the reason. The last thing that women in abusive relationships need is to be told that they can turn a bad man good by marrying him. Women in abusive relationships need help getting out, not a prod to stay in.

Rape Is Caused by a Culture of Toxic Masculinity

Jaclyn Friedman

Jaclyn Friedman is the executive director of Women, Action, and the Media and the author of What You Really Really Want: The Smart Girl's Shame-Free Guide to Sex and Safety.

Last summer, two young football players in the Ohio town of Steubenville carried the unconscious body of a local girl from party to party, violating her in ways you'd probably prefer not to think about. (I'm not pretending this incident is merely "alleged," because there's video and this column isn't a court of law.) Today [March 13, 2013], she'll face her attackers in court for the first time. It's a brave act, as she surely knows she'll not only be facing down the boys who did this to her, but also the adults whose jobs it is to blame her and call her a liar. Only she can know what will make this sacrifice worthwhile: Is it enough for her to be heard in court? Will it only be healing if the boys are convicted? Whatever it is she needs, I hope she gets it.

A Toxic Masculinity

But rape prosecutions are argued on behalf of the state, not just the victim, and there's a good reason: Rape doesn't just harm one person. It tears at the fabric of our communities. And if we treat this trial as simply the story of what a couple of kids did to another, we're missing the point. This isn't an isolated incident, and the incident itself didn't happen in isolation.

Jaclyn Friedman, "Toxic Masculinity," *American Prospect*, March 13, 2013. Copyright © 2013 American Prospect. All rights reserved. Reproduced with permission.

This rape is like most in that it was enabled by a deeply entrenched, toxic masculinity. It's a masculinity that defines itself not only in opposition to female-ness, but as inherently superior, drawing its strength from dominance over women's "weakness," and creating men who are happy to deliberately undermine women's power; it is only in opposition to female vulnerability that it can be strong. Or, as former NFL quarterback and newly-minted feminist Don McPherson recently put it, "We don't raise boys to be men. We raise them not to be women, or gay men." This starts in childhood for many boys, who are taught young that they'll be punished for doing anything "girly," from playing with dolls to crying, or even preferring to read over "rough housing" outside.

You can bet that any customs that require impunity for violence against women are built on toxic masculinity.

Toxic masculinity has its fingerprints all over the Steubenville case. The violence done to the victim was born out of the boys' belief that a) sexually dominating a helpless girl's body made them powerful and cool, and b) there would be no consequences for them because of their status as star athletes. The defense is basing their entire case on it, arguing that this near- (and sometimes totally) unconscious girl's body was the boys' to use because "she didn't affirmatively say no." The football community's response—by which I mean not just the coaches, school, and players, but the entire community of fans—is steeped in the assumptions of toxic masculinity, treating the athletes and the game as more important than some silly girl's right to both bodily autonomy and justice. Steubenville residents have been quick to rally around the team, suggesting that the victim "put herself in a position to be violated" and refusing to talk to police investigating the assault. The two players who cooperated with police were suspended from the football team, while the players accused of the rape have been allowed to play. The coach even went so far as to threaten a *New York Times* reporter asking questions about the case. (No surprise there: When it comes to male-dominated sports, toxic masculinity is the rule, not the exception.)

But sports is hardly the only breeding ground for toxic masculinity. Witness the recent, vicious bullying of Zerlina Maxwell by fans of Fox News. Last week, Maxwell was on Hannity and dared to opine that the best rape prevention isn't about what women can do to protect themselves, but instead focuses on raising men who don't rape. She also personally identified herself as a survivor of rape. What followed was a nearly inconceivable onslaught of misogynist and racist attacks, including repeated threats of rape and death. All because a black woman insisted that the work of stopping rape— "women's work" if there ever was such a thing—requires men's labor. Under the influence of toxic masculinity, the logical response to a man being forced or even encouraged to do something coded "female" is always violence.

The U.N. is in the midst of its 57th Commission on the Status of Women, this year focusing on gendered violence, a global pandemic made all the more urgent by growing evidence that social change leads to increased violence against women. Why? Because destabilizing established social order— even in the interest of what we might agree is progress—can leave people feeling vulnerable. And when men feel vulnerable, toxic masculinity teaches them the way to reassert their power is by dominating women. There's a pall hanging over the proceedings, a real risk that this year's commission may wind up like last year's, failing to come to any policy agreements thanks to the obstructionism of a handful of patriarchal countries who claim that their traditional and religious customs would be infringed upon if they had to take action to end gendered violence in their countries. You can bet that any customs that require impunity for violence against women are built on toxic masculinity.

The Need for Intervention

It's time for a serious intervention in masculinity. It's not enough to not be a rapist. You don't get a cookie or a Nobel Peace Prize for that. If we want to end the pandemic of rape, it's going to require an entire global movement of men who are willing to do the hard work required to unpack and interrogate the ideas of masculinity they were raised with, and to create and model new masculinities that don't enable misogyny. Masculinities built not on power over women, but on power with women.

If the rest of us shift our relationship to masculinity, ideas like "she was asking for it" ... won't make sense anymore.

This is going to take real work, which is why so many men resist it. It requires destabilizing your own identity, and giving up attitudes and behaviors from which you're used to deriving power, likely before you learn how to derive power from other, more just and productive places. There are real risks for men who challenge toxic masculinity, from social shaming to actual "don't be a fag" violence—punishments that won't ease until many, many men take the plunge. But there are great rewards to be had, too, beyond stopping rape. Toxic masculinity is damaging to men, too, positing them as stoic sex-and-violence machines with allergies to tenderness, playfulness, and vulnerability. A reinvented masculinity will surely give men more room to express and explore themselves without shame or fear. (It will also, not incidentally, reduce rape against men as well, because many rapes of men are committed by other men with the intention of "feminizing"—that is, humiliating through dominance—their victim.)

These interventions start with a "feminine" activity: introspection. What did you learn about "being a man," from whom? How are those lessons working out for you, and for the people you love and your communities? Taking action can be as simple as men publicly owning their preference for "female" coded things, whether that's child-rearing, nonviolence, feminism, or anything else—and being willing to suffer the social consequences. It can be more formal, working with established organizations like Men Stopping Violence. As more men take responsibility for the work, it will surely also take on forms no one has yet envisioned.

The Role of Men

Obviously, the mouth-breathing troglodytes who hailed hate down on Maxwell aren't going to be interested in this project. And there's strong evidence that most rapes are committed by repeat offenders who may not call what they're doing by the r-word, but know full-well they don't have their partner's consent. Remaking masculinity isn't about sweetly beseeching those guys until they don "This is What a Feminist Looks Like" t-shirts. It's about two much more practical things: 1) raising new generations of boys much less likely to grow into rapists and/or Fox trolls, and, meanwhile, 2) undermining the social license to operate which allows the current generation of assholes to keep trolling and raping with impunity.

In other words: What if misogynist trolling got you shunned by their friends and family? What if raping someone was actually likely to result in your expulsion from your team, and your conviction in court? If the rest of us shift our relationship to masculinity, ideas like "she was asking for it" or "don't be a pussy" won't make sense anymore, and the guys who try to cling to them will find themselves isolated, facing serious social and legal consequences.

There's already some sign that this can work, and that the work is underway. Vancouver's new initiative placing the focus on preventing offenders, not victims, is showing early promise. The Feminist Wire just launched a "Masculinities Forum" to create a more explicit dialogue on just these issues. And the organization Breakthrough has launched a global "Ring The Bell" campaign that is poised to take the lead on this very issue, calling for one million men to take concrete action to end violence against women.

It's not a moment too soon. Just as putting the onus on women to prevent their own rapes on an individual basis is both wrong and ineffective, so too is putting the onus on women to stop rape as a social phenomenon. It's time to "sack up" and step up, men. I promise it will hurt you a lot less than it's hurting me.

Editor's Note: On May 17, the two young football players were adjudicated delinquent of rape, comparable to a guilty verdict in adult criminal court.

Rape Is Not Caused by Patriarchy and Is Not Normal

Wendy McElroy

Wendy McElroy is a research fellow at the Independent Institute and a contributing editor to Ideas on Liberty, The New Libertarian, Free Inquiry, *and* Liberty *magazines.*

A pivot point occurred within feminism on the issue of rape in 1975 when the book *Against Our Will: Men, Women and Rape* by Susan Brownmiller appeared. In its pages, Brownmiller attempted to chart the history of rape from the Neanderthal through to modern man, placing great emphasis on periods of war and crisis. *Against Our Will* reportedly gave rape its history. It became a founding document of the "rape culture," which further propelled the feminist movement from liberalism to political correctness [PC], which has also been called gender or radical feminism.

Myths About Rape

In her book, Brownmiller maintained that rape is the primary mechanism through which men subjugate women. "Man's discovery that his genitalia could serve as a weapon to generate fear must rank as one of the most important discoveries of prehistoric times, along with the use of fire, and the first crude stone ax. From prehistoric times to the present, I believe, rape has played a critical function. It is nothing more or less than a conscious process of intimidation by which *all* men keep *all* women in a state of fear." [Emphasis in the original.]

Wendy McElroy, "Three Myths of Rape that Need Sunlight," *Daily Bell*, February 19, 2015. Copyright © 2015 The Daily Bell. All rights reserved. Reproduced with permission.

Some of today's most prevalent myths about rape were cemented into the culture by Brownmiller. In particular, Brownmiller presented three interrelated myths:

1. rape is a part of patriarchy;

2. men have created a "mass psychology" of rape; and,

3. rape is a part of "normal" life.

I dispute each one of them.

Regarding patriarchy, suffice it to say, those who promote the concept [that rape is a product of patriarchy] need to ignore many facts.

[Note: This article addresses the origin of myths and terms that still wield great influence within feminism, academia, politics and our culture. Some concepts have evolved or expanded in meaning. "Patriarchy" is an example; there is currently a debate on whether all men benefit from "white male culture" or whether the "patriarchy" refers to internal social structures that can oppress people regardless of their gender. Other concepts have not drifted far from their origin. In both cases, it is not possible to understand the current expression of ideas without some understanding of their roots.]

Rape Is a Part of Patriarchy

The word "patriarchy" is Greek and means "rule of the father." Adrienne Rich—a key philosopher of PC feminism—offered what has become a fairly standard definition of "patriarchy" in her book *Of Woman Born* (1977): "Patriarchy is the power of the fathers: a familial—social, ideological, political system in which men—by force, direct pressure or through ritual, tradition, law, and language, customs, etiquette, education, and the division of labor, determine what part women should or shall not play, and in which the female is everywhere subsumed under the male."

The definition is often expanded to include capitalism as an aspect of patriarchy. This reflects the input of highly influential theorists like Catherine MacKinnon who referred to PC feminism as "post-Marxist." She meant that PC feminism largely accepted the Marxism context but not its claim that economic status determined class affiliation. Gender was the salient factor. Men, as a class, had constructed institutions, such as the free market and the traditional family, which needed to be deconstructed.

Refuting the concept of a North American patriarchy needs its own book; this column deals with patriarchy in passing and points to more plausible causes of rape. Regarding patriarchy, suffice it to say, those who promote the concept need to ignore many facts. For example, men and women are victims of domestic violence at virtually the same rate; men constitute the vast majority of prisoners; if prison populations are included, men and women are probably raped at virtually the same rate; they are far more likely to be murdered or die in war; anti-male violence by women is accepted in the popular culture and often causes laughter.

If Brownmiller wishes to argue for a continuum of male oppression, she cannot chose only the fiction, historical tidbits and anecdotes that favor her.

If not patriarchy, what *does* explain rape? A casualty of this myth has been research. Studies on the causes (plural) of rape have almost dried up because—as any right thinking person knows—there is only one cause: patriarchy. During the heyday of liberal feminism and sexual curiosity, research was more sophisticated. In their book, *The Crime and Consequences of Rape* (1982), Charles W. Dean, Mary de Bruyn-Kops, [and] Charles C. Thomas, reported, "The Kinsey study, begun in the 1950s and completed after Kinsey's death by Gebhard and associates, classified seven types of rapists: assaultive, amoral, drunken, explosive, double-standard, mental defective and psychotic. . . ."

People murder for money, for love, out of jealousy or patriotism—the rationalizations go on and on. Rape is every bit as complex. Men *and women* rape because of sexual hunger, a need to prove themselves, hatred of women or a desire for revenge, as a political statement or from peer pressure (as in gang rapes). Men *and women* rape from a constellation of complicated motives, which become further blurred when there is alcohol or drug use.

But it is no longer proper to suggest that there could be as many motives for rape as there are for other violent crimes. Other explanations for rape are defined out of possibility.

Men Have Created a "Mass Psychology" of Rape

Brownmiller's second myth is that men have created a mass psychology of rape. Throughout the book, Brownmiller dips in and out of history, selecting whatever supports her statement. Some references have little to no connection with reality. For example, she quotes from fiction works. She also points to historical evidence that is difficult to credit. When Brownmiller speaks of *prehistoric* man as the beginning of man's use of "his genitalia . . . as a weapon," for example, the reader is left to wonder where she acquired her amazing knowledge of Neanderthals and their sexual attitudes.

Contradicting references are dismissed in passing, if mentioned at all. At one point, Brownmiller notes, "People often ask what the classic Greek myths reveal about rape. Actually, they reveal very little. . . ." Yet these myths are widely held to be archetypes of human psychology. If Brownmiller wishes to argue for a continuum of male oppression, she cannot chose only the fiction, historical tidbits and anecdotes that favor her.

Yet, even with a careful sifting of history and fiction, Brownmiller's evidence does not support her conclusion: namely, that rape "is nothing more or less than a conscious process of intimidation by which *all* men keep *all* women in a state of fear." To punch up the argument, she introduces statistics that allegedly "prove" the mass psychology of rape.

But let me take the inflated statistics at face value. A rape rate of 25% means that 75% of women will not be raped. Even assuming a one-to-one correlation between victims and rapists—that is, assuming no serial rapists—this means 75% of men will never rape. Indeed, many men would come to the defense of an attacked woman.

The foregoing math may seem obvious. But the claim of a "mass psychology of rape" or a "rape culture" makes it necessary to state the obvious. And it raises a question. What other group in our culture could be castigated in this manner without a backlash? If all blacks or bisexuals were accused of being sadists or benefiting from sadism, people would howl in protest.

Arguing from the extreme, Brownmiller draws conclusions about the normal. This is a fallacy.

And lest a single man escape rape accusations by pleading that he had never contemplated committing the act, Brownmiller explains how good intentions and good behavior do not exonerate him. "Once we accept as basic truth that rape is not a crime of irrational, impulsive, uncontrollable lust, but is a deliberate, hostile, violent act of degradation and possession on the part of a would-be conqueror, designed to intimidate and inspire fear, we must look toward those elements in our culture that promote and propagandize these attitudes, which offer men ... the ideology and psychological encouragement to commit their acts of aggression *without awareness, for the most part, that they have committed a punishable crime,* let alone a moral wrong." [Italics in original.]

Brownmiller is correct. If we accept her position "as basic truth," then her conclusions follow. But such a theory allows for no contradictory evidence. There is no possibility—through action, thought or word—for a man to escape the charge of rape. It becomes axiomatically and ideologically true.

Rape Is a Part of "Normal" Life

Brownmiller's third myth is that rape is part of normal life. To reach this conclusion, Brownmiller makes great leaps of logic. For example, chapter after chapter of *Against Our Will* dwells upon rape during times of war and severe societal turmoil. Because men rape in times of war and upheaval, she concludes that rape is part of "normal" life. But the very circumstances highlighted are not expressions of normal life but evidence of its breakdown. Arguing from the extreme, Brownmiller draws conclusions about the normal. This is a fallacy. It is akin to concluding, "men kill in war; therefore, peacetime murder is the norm."

Against Our Will arrives at the third myth via ideological bias, not empirical research. Although Brownmiller's book is sometimes taken for a chronicle of historical fact, a strong political slant underlies the presentation of those cherry-picked facts. Consider Brownmiller's opinion of private property: "Concepts of hierarchy, slavery and private property flowed from, and could only be predicated upon, the initial subjugation of woman."

In her book *Sexual Personae*, the self-identified "dissident" feminist Camille Paglia offered a more plausible relationship between society and rape. Paglia writes, "Generation after generation, men must be educated, refined, and ethically persuaded away from their tendency toward anarchy and brutishness. Society is not the enemy, as feminism ignorantly claims. Society is woman's protection against rape."

I dispute whether men or women have a natural tendency toward Hobbesian brutishness. But I believe normal society protects against violence of all kinds, including rape. For one thing, normal society enforces rules against violence, which often penalize perpetrators through imprisonment, social sanctions, reparations or restitution.

Myths about rape harm men, women and the victims of rape both male and female. Goodwill between the sexes has been replaced with rage or resentment, and for no productive purpose. Rape is not a part of patriarchy; like all crime, it is a lamentable choice that some people make for their individual reasons. Men have not created a "mass psychology" of rape; PC feminists have created a mass fear about rape. Rape is not a part of "normal" life; normal life helps to protect men and women against rape.

CHAPTER 3

Has Legislation to Reduce Violence Against Women Been Effective?

Overview: The Violence Against Women Act

Lisa N. Sacco

Lisa N. Sacco is an analyst in illicit drugs and crime policy at the Congressional Research Service.

VAWA [Violence Against Women Act] was originally passed by Congress as part of the broader Violent Crime Control and Law Enforcement Act of 1994. The Violence Against Women Act of 1994 (1) enhanced investigations and prosecutions of sex offenses and (2) provided for a number of grant programs to address the issue of violence against women from a variety of angles, including law enforcement, public and private entities and service providers, and victims of crime. The sections below highlight examples of these VAWA provisions.

Investigations and Prosecutions

As passed in 1994, VAWA impacted federal investigations and prosecutions of cases involving violence against women in a number of ways. For instance, it established new offenses and penalties for the violation of a protection order as well as stalking in which an abuser crossed a state line to injure or harass another, or forced a victim to cross a state line under duress and then physically harmed the victim in the course of a violent crime. It added new provisions to require states and territories to enforce protection orders issued by other states, tribes, and territories. VAWA also allowed for enhanced sentencing of repeat federal sex offenders. It also authorized funding for the Attorney General to develop training programs to assist probation and parole officers in working with released sex offenders.

Lisa N. Sacco, "The Violence Against Women Act: Overview, Legislation, and Federal Funding," Congressional Research Service, R42499, March 6, 2014, pp. 2–4, 9, 14–16. Courtesy of Congressional Research Service.

In addition, VAWA established a new requirement for pre-trial detention in federal sex offense or child pornography felony cases. It also modified the Federal Rules of Evidence to include new procedures specifying that, with few exceptions, a victim's past sexual behavior was not admissible in federal criminal and civil cases of sexual misconduct. In addition, VAWA asked the Attorney General to study measures in place to ensure confidentiality between sexual assault or domestic violence victims and their counselors.

VAWA created a number of grant programs for a range of activities.

VAWA mandated restitution to victims of specified federal sex offenses, specifically sexual abuse as well as sexual exploitation and other abuse of children. It also established new provisions, including a civil remedy that allows victims of sexual assault to seek civil penalties from their alleged assailants, and a provision that allows rape victims to demand that their alleged assailants be tested for the HIV virus.

Grant Programs

VAWA created a number of grant programs for a range of activities, including programs aimed at (1) preventing domestic violence and related crimes; (2) encouraging collaboration among law enforcement, judicial personnel, and public/private sector providers with respect to services for victims of domestic violence and related crimes; (3) investigating and prosecuting domestic violence and related crimes; and (4) addressing the needs of individuals in a special population group (e.g., elderly, disabled, children and youth, individuals of ethnic and racial communities, and nonimmigrant women). VAWA grants are administered by the Department of Justice, Office on Violence Against Women and Office of Justice Programs as well as by the Department of Health and Human Services, Centers for Disease Control and Prevention.

Under VAWA, grants were authorized for capital improvements to prevent crime in public transportation systems as well as in public and national parks. It also expanded the Family Violence Prevention and Services Act (FVPSA) to include grants for youth education on domestic violence and intimate partner violence as well as to include grants for community intervention and prevention programs.

As mentioned, VAWA provided for federal grants to state, local, and tribal law enforcement entities to investigate and prosecute violent crimes against women. It established an additional grant to bolster investigations and prosecutions in rural areas. It also established a grant program to encourage state, local, and tribal arrest policies in domestic violence cases.

VAWA authorized grants for education and training for judges and court personnel in state and federal courts on the laws of rape, sexual assault, domestic violence, and other crimes of violence motivated by the victim's gender. It also authorized grants to assist state and local governments in entering data on stalking and domestic violence into national databases.

Since it was enacted in 1994, Congress has reauthorized VAWA three times.

VAWA authorized the expansion of grants under the Public Health Service Act to include rape prevention education. Additionally, it expanded the purposes of the Runaway and Homeless Youth Act to allow for grant funding to assist youth at risk of (or who have been subjected to) sexual abuse. VAWA reauthorized the Court-Appointed Special Advocate Program and the Child Abuse Training Programs for Judicial Personnel and Practitioners. It also authorized funding for Grants for Televised Testimony by Victims of Child Abuse.

VAWA established the National Domestic Violence Hotline and authorized funding for its operation. It also authorized funding for battered women's shelters, in addition to including special protections for battered nonimmigrant women and children. . . .

Since it was enacted in 1994, Congress has reauthorized VAWA three times. Of note, the reauthorizations in 2000 and 2005 had broad bipartisan support while the most recent reauthorization in 2013 faced some adversity. . . .

New Provisions for American Indian Tribes, Nonimmigrants, and Underserved Populations

VAWA 2013 included new provisions for American Indian tribes. It granted authority to Indian tribes to exercise special domestic violence criminal jurisdiction and civil jurisdiction to issue and enforce protection orders over any person, and created a new grant program to assist Indian tribes in exercising special criminal jurisdiction over cases involving domestic violence. It created a voluntary two-year pilot program for Indian tribes that make a request to the Attorney General to be designated as a participating tribe to have *special domestic violence criminal jurisdiction* over such cases.

VAWA 2013 also expanded the purpose areas of grants to tribal governments and coalitions to include sex trafficking. Additionally, it expanded the purpose areas of grants for American Indian tribal governments and coalitions to develop and promote legislation and policies that enhance best practices for responding to violent crimes against Indian women. It also expanded the purpose areas of grants for American Indian tribal coalitions to raise awareness of and response to domestic violence to include identifying and providing technical assistance to enhance access to services for Indian women victims of domestic and sexual violence, including sex trafficking.

The most recent reauthorization of VAWA extended VAWA coverage to derivative children whose self-petitioning parent died during the petition process, a benefit currently afforded to foreign nationals under the family-based provisions of the Immigration and Naturalization Act (INA). It also exempted VAWA self-petitioners, U visa petitioners, and battered foreign nationals from being classified as inadmissible for legal permanent resident status if their financial circumstances raised concerns about them becoming potential public charges. Additionally, it amended the INA to expand the definition of the nonimmigrant U visa to include victims of stalking.

VAWA 2013 added housing rights for victims of domestic violence, dating violence, sexual assault, and stalking.

VAWA 2013 added several new purpose areas of the Grants to Encourage Arrest Policies and Enforcement of Protection Orders program (Arrest Program), one of which was to improve the criminal justice system response to immigrant victims of domestic violence, sexual assault, dating violence, and stalking.

Underserved Populations

In addition to expanding the definition of "underserved populations," VAWA 2013 established several new grant provisions to address the needs of underserved populations. It required STOP implementation plans to include demographic data on the distribution of underserved populations within states and how states will meet the needs of their underserved populations. It also expanded the purpose areas of the Grants to Combat Violent Crimes on Campuses program to address the needs of underserved populations on college campuses. It amended a previously unfunded VAWA program, Grants for Outreach to Underserved Populations, to ensure that it would receive funding by allotting 2% of annual appropriated funding for the Arrest and STOP programs to the Grants for Outreach to Underserved Populations program.

New Requirements for Housing and Higher Education

VAWA 2013 added housing rights for victims of domestic violence, dating violence, sexual assault, and stalking, including a provision that states that an applicant may not be denied public housing assistance on the basis that the person has been a victim of domestic violence, dating violence, sexual assault, or stalking. Under the Transitional Housing Assistance Grant program, it ensured that victims receiving transitional housing assistance are not subject to prohibited activities, including background checks or clinical evaluations, to determine eligibility for services. It removed the requirement that victims must be "fleeing" from a violence situation in order to receive transitional housing assistance. VAWA 2013 also specified that transitional housing services may include assisting victims in seeking employment.

VAWA 2013 required each executive department carrying out a covered housing program to adopt a model emergency transfer plan to use in allowing tenants who are victims of domestic violence, dating violence, sexual assault, or stalking to transfer to another available and safe dwelling unit of assisted housing. It also required the Secretary of Housing and Urban Development to establish policies and procedures under which a victim requesting such a transfer may receive Section 8 assistance under the U.S. Housing Act of 1937.

VAWA 2013 amended the Higher Education Act of 1965 (HEA) and established new mandatory grant guidelines for institutions of higher education in their incident response procedures and development of programs to prevent domestic violence, sexual assault, stalking, and dating violence. VAWA 2013 also addressed mandatory crime reporting and safety procedures on college campuses. For example, it amended the HEA to ensure that crime statistics on individuals who were "intentionally selected" because of their national origin or gender identity are recorded and reported according to category of prejudice.

The Violence Against Women Act Has Reduced Violence

The White House

The White House communicates the official policies of the President of the United States.

Before VAWA [Violence Against Women Act], federal law never attempted to use its full potential to reach violence against women. There were no major grant programs specifically focused on violence against women. And, as in many states, the federal criminal law did not give parity to this violence—while the federal law had been used to cover a large range of criminal offenses that elude the states (where interstate travel is concerned), there was no attempt to use this power to target violence against women. Because most crimes remain subject to state jurisdiction, VAWA aimed to inject equal treatment into the state system by providing an "unprecedented" number of programs geared toward helping local law enforcement banish myths about rape and battering. Meanwhile, at the federal level, it created new offenses for battering, rape, and stalking using federal interstate jurisdiction.

Breaking the Taboo

If there was one thing that we knew in 1990, it was that false, and often sexist, beliefs about this violence distorted our criminal justice system. Was it any wonder that the system had such low reporting rates for rape and domestic violence, when many Americans did not think them crimes at all? In a 1975 national survey, 28% of respondents agreed that slapping a spouse was "necessary," "normal" or "good."

The White House, "1 Is 2 Many: Twenty Years Fighting Violence Against Women and Girls," September 2014, pp. 16–20. Courtesy of the Office of the Vice President.

Thankfully, over the years, these attitudes have changed. A 2006 study showed that 97% of college students surveyed agreed that for a husband to use physical force to make his wife have sex would constitute intimate partner violence. Today, a majority of men report that they have a family member or friend that they believe has been a victim of domestic violence or sexual assault. On the other hand, pockets of resistance remain: we know that rape myths and victim-blaming continue to exist in the larger community and in the criminal justice system, both at home and abroad.

> The original VAWA ... extended federal power to treat domestic violence and sexual assault similar to other federal crimes.

When VAWA was first drafted, it was difficult to get a sense of the scope of the problem—data was conflicting if non-existent. After VAWA was passed, then-Senator [Joe] Biden pushed to create an Office on Violence Against Women within the Department of Justice to ensure that there was an institution devoted to this problem embedded within our federal justice system. Over the years, that Office has consistently identified needs and distributed funds to state and local programs, using a smart, targeted approach. In partnership with other agencies, this focus has developed promising practices and yielded several landmark studies, including the 2010 CDC [Centers for Disease Control and Prevention] Report on Intimate Partner Violence.

Extending Federal Power

In 1994, gaps existed in federal protections normally granted victims of other serious crimes. It is unlawful for most felons to possess a gun—but these provisions did not necessarily address violence against women. When VAWA was first passed in 1994, Congress made it a federal crime to possess a firearm or ammunition while subject to a valid permanent protection order for harassing, stalking, or threatening an intimate partner. A 1996 amendment to the Gun Control Act extended the ban on firearm possession to individuals convicted of a qualifying misdemeanor crime of domestic violence, even if the conviction occurred before the date of the law's enactment.

Not surprisingly, when VAWA was first passed, almost every state crime involving interstate elements (from gun crimes to cattle rustling) was covered by the federal criminal code—but not sexual assault and domestic violence. As then-Senator Biden said in 1992, if you can take a cow across state lines and commit a federal felony, then the same treatment was due crimes disproportionately affecting women.

The original VAWA thus extended federal power to treat domestic violence and sexual assault similar to other federal crimes. For example, the first federal prosecution under these laws involved a husband who severely beat his wife. For five days, he drove her in and out of West Virginia before taking her to a hospital in Kentucky. The Fourth Circuit upheld the law as within traditional federal criminal jurisdiction. This set a decisive precedent that combatting violence against women is, literally, *the federal government's business.* Since then, there have been hundreds of cases filed and 175 convictions obtained. In reauthorizing VAWA, Congress has expanded these interstate provisions to cover cyberstalking and crimes committed in federal maritime and territorial jurisdiction.

Civic Groups Working Together

One of VAWA's key legal innovations focused on incentivizing cooperation between civic groups otherwise at war. Rather than a stick, the law provided a carrot: if police and prosecutors worked together with advocates, they could receive seed money for their cooperative efforts. The money could be used to train law enforcement or to provide victims assistance and strengthen local nonprofits, but only on condition of cooperative effort. To obtain a grant, a state had to certify that it provided a basic level of legal protections and that it would use the formula grants to coordinate the community's response.

Sex crimes are extremely unique because of the preconceived ideas, notions, bias that no other crime victim experiences.

The coordinated community response model (CCR) is one of the hallmarks of the Violence Against Women Act. Evidence shows that efforts to address violence against women are particularly effective when they are combined and integrated across various disciplines. Participants in a CCR ideally include law enforcement agencies, advocates, health care providers, and child protection services. CCRs may also work with local businesses and employers, the media, and clergy, and often engage the entire community in efforts to change the social norms and attitudes that contribute to violence against women. Studies show that these programs have increased both arrests and prosecutions in sexual assault and domestic violence cases. Along the way, they have helped to defuse myths and inequalities and reduce the effects of violence against women.

On average, VAWA funds help to train over 500,000 law enforcement officers, prosecutors, judges, victim advocates, and other personnel every year. Ongoing training may help police officers to better understand victim behavior. For instance, before being trained, many law enforcement professionals shared the common misconception that stranger rape is more common than date rape, or that date rape is somehow less traumatic. Law enforcement or legal system personnel may ask why victims don't "just" leave, even though that might be the most dangerous time for the victim of domestic violence. They may believe, contrary to fact, that all rapes involve physical injury or that most victims make a prompt complaint.

Law enforcement has come to recognize that these myths may imperil lives and encourage offenders. As one former law enforcement officer notes:

> "I think sex crimes are extremely unique because of the pre-conceived ideas, notions, bias that no other crime victim experiences.... Imagine the power that sex offenders experience because victims weren't being believed or because they weren't being given the support they needed to participate in the criminal justice system."

A national law enforcement report adds: untrained police officers may not be aware that:

> "A victim's first contact with law enforcement rarely happens after the first or even the second domestic violence incident," but rather may only occur "after the pattern of abuse is well established and the level of physical injury has become serious."

The Progress Made

Specialization has proved a powerful tool in improving the criminal justice response to violence against women. VAWA funding supports law enforcement and prosecution units that deal exclusively with domestic violence or sexual assault, and often with remarkable results. Specialized domestic violence police units collect evidence in a much higher percentage of cases than traditional patrol units. The evidence collected by specialized units is more likely to be useful for prosecution, leading to higher rates of prosecution, conviction, and sentencing. Specialized prosecution units also make a difference: from 2008 to 2012, a study of 50–60 VAWA-funded prosecutors' offices showed that they accepted for prosecution a remarkable 73% of sexual assault cases.

Evidence suggests that specialization is also important in court systems. Domestic violence courts process cases more efficiently, increase offender compliance, impose enhanced penalties, improve outcomes for victims, and achieve higher rates of conviction. One study found that 75% of victims said they would be more likely to report future violence if a domestic violence court were available to them.

Tragically, intimate partner violence can escalate and lead to death. Although the rate of intimate partner homicides has decreased since the passage of VAWA, there is a long way to go before we reach zero. In one hopeful development, some communities are adopting methods to predict which abusers pose the greatest threats. After applying one lethality assessment tool, Maryland witnessed a 34% drop in intimate partner homicides. Inspired by the tragic domestic violence homicide of a client, Newburyport, Massachusetts created one of the first high risk teams in the country and identified over 100 high risk victims during its first six years of operation from 2005 to 2011. Since the formation of the team, there have been zero domestic violence homicides reported in the community.

In 2013, Vice President Biden and Attorney General [Eric] Holder announced VAWA funding for twelve communities to replicate these projects. VAWA 2013 took additional steps in this direction, by requiring states to develop goals and activities to reduce domestic violence homicides and integrating homicide reduction into key VAWA grant programs. Jurisdictions in 31 states have begun using lethality assessment tools, but there is an urgent need to make more progress.

Two Decades of Legislation Have Improved Violence Against Women

Tara Culp-Ressler

Tara Culp-Ressler is the health editor for ThinkProgress.

The 20th anniversary of the Violence Against Women Act [VAWA]—landmark legislation that was signed into law by President [Bill] Clinton on September 13, 1994—comes at a particularly prescient moment, as the country is engaged in a national conversation about the NFL's responsibility to adequately respond to incidences of domestic abuse perpetrated by its football players.

As all attention has been focused on the video of former Baltimore Ravens running back Ray Rice punching his then-fiancee in a hotel elevator, as well as the NFL's botched response to the surveillance tape evidence, it can be hard to feel like the country is taking any meaningful steps toward taking violence against women seriously. But, while there's certainly a lot of work left to be done, the national legislation aimed at supporting victims of domestic violence has changed the landscape in some significant ways.

The Progress Made

Here's a look at how we've progressed in the past two decades:

We have more resources to address and prevent domestic abuse.

The whole point of VAWA is to provide more institutional resources for domestic violence victims. In order to accomplish that, the law expanded the network of rape crisis centers

Tara Culp-Ressler, "How the Country Has Changed Under the Violence Against Women Act," *ThinkProgress*, September 12, 2014. Copyright © 2014 ThinkProgress. All rights reserved. Reproduced with permission.

and domestic violence shelters across the country, as well as established the National Domestic Violence Hotline. VAWA also provides funding for efforts to prevent crime, like expanding youth education programs to teach kids about what constitutes dating violence, implementing safety measures on public transportation, and requiring the government to conduct more research into domestic violence so we'll have a better understanding of the scope of the problem.

Violence against women is no longer considered to be a "private family matter," and is now widely regarded as something that requires a public solution.

Fewer people are becoming victims of violence.

According to data from the Department of Justice, domestic violence rates declined 64 percent between 1993 and 2010. And the rate of women being murdered by men in single victim/single offender situations—often characteristic of intimate partner violence—dropped by 26 percent over a similar time period, between 1996 and 2012. One study attempting to figure out why domestic violence rates dropped so dramatically in the 1990s attributed the decline partly to VAWA, which "has been an important impetus for funding in the area of civil legal assistance."

We're more comfortable talking about domestic abuse.

"Even just 20 years ago, violence against women in America was an epidemic few people wanted to talk about, let alone do something about," Vice President Joe Biden, who introduced VAWA and has championed the legislation ever since, pointed out in an op-ed published this week [September 2014] to mark VAWA's anniversary. But that's slowly started to change. Victims are becoming more comfortable reaching out; the National Domestic Violence Hotline has received over 3 million calls since 1996, and 92 percent of those callers say it's their first call for help. Violence against women is no longer considered to be a "private family matter," and is now widely regarded as something that requires a public solution. According to the advocacy group Futures Without Violence, before the 1980s, there were about 150 articles in major newspapers covering the issue of domestic violence. In the decades of the 2000s, there were more than 7,000.

We're better at recognizing the diversity of survivors' experiences.

The latest iteration of VAWA made some important updates to the original 1994 law. It expanded protections for Native American women by giving tribes more authority to prosecute domestic abuse, protected LGBT individuals from being discriminated against in shelters, and ensured that immigrants' legal status can't be exploited by their abusers. It also expanded the definition of violence to specifically include crimes like cyberstalking. Those new provisions were a sticking point for many Republicans, who refused to pass the expanded version VAWA in 2013 and allowed the law to lapse in the first time since its 1994 passage. Last February, Congress finally reauthorized VAWA with the protections for diverse groups of victims intact.

We've enacted more legal protections for victims.

Before VAWA, we didn't have a criminal justice system that was set up to handle these issues. Sexual assault and domestic violence weren't even included in the federal criminal code. VAWA strengthened the federal punishments for those crimes—which led the way for states to reform their own laws in this area so that, for example, spousal rape is now treated just as seriously as stranger rape across the country. VAWA funds also train over 500,000 law enforcement officers, prosecutors, and judges every year so they'll be able to better respond to cases involving intimate partner violence, abuse, and assault. And, thanks to the federal legislation, victims' past sexual behavior is not admissible in trials where they're accusing someone else of sexual misconduct.

Laws Against Violence Help but Enforcement Is Needed

Ruth Rosen

Ruth Rosen is professor emeritus of history at University of California, Davis, and author of The World Split Open: How the Modern Women's Movement Changed America.

Until the women's movement organized in the late 1960s and early 1970s, most Americans considered wife beating a custom. The police ignored what went on behind closed doors and women hid their bruises beneath layers of make-up. Like rape or abortion, wife beating was viewed as a private and shameful act which few women discussed. Many battered victims, moreover, felt they "deserved" to be beaten—because they acted too uppity, didn't get dinner on the table on time, or couldn't silence their children's shouts and screams.

Men slugged women with impunity until feminist activists renamed wife beating as domestic violence, and described its victims as "battered women." Such women needed refuge, and activists created a network of shelters for women who tried to escape, often with their children, the violence threatened by their partners.

The Violence Against Women Act

Throughout the 1970s, feminists sought to teach women that they had the right to be free of violence. *"We will not be beaten"* became the slogan of the movement against domestic violence. Books and pamphlets argued that violence violated women's rights. But it wasn't until 1994, during the Presidency of Bill Clinton, that Congress passed the Violence Against Women Act [VAWA], legislation that allocated funds to inves-

Ruth Rosen, "We Will Not Be Beaten," *openDemocracy*, September 8, 2014. Copyright © 2014 openDemocracy. All rights reserved. Reproduced with permission.

tigate crimes against women, created shelters for battered women, provided legal aid, and protected victims evicted from their homes because of domestic violence.

Like abortion, VAWA symbolized women's new social, economic, and sexual independence from men's control.

Feminists considered VAWA landmark legislation. It gave the federal government the authority to punish domestic violence. Studies showed that the law had some positive impact by creating refuges and forcing the judicial system to deal with domestic violence. But as daily newspapers reported, it didn't stop violence against women in private or in public—at home, at universities, on streets and in parks.

Nor did it take long for right-wing opponents to try and weaken VAWA. As an increasingly polarized America bitterly fought over women's new rights and protections, social conservatives targeted the VAWA as undermining the traditional family and men's dominant role in society. And each time the legislation came up for reauthorisation, activists had to renew their struggle to protect what they had gained, even as they tried to expand VAWA to include new groups of women. In 2013 for example, opponents wanted to deny Native American, same-sex couples, and immigrant women, the protections provided from VAWA. They lost, but only after a lengthy Congressional political battle.

Setbacks were of course inevitable. Like abortion, VAWA symbolized women's new social, economic, and sexual independence from men's control. In 2000, a sharply divided Supreme Court, in *United States v. Morrison*, struck down a section of the VAWA that gave women the right to sue their attackers. By a 5-4 majority, the court overturned the provision as unconstitutional because it usurped Congress's power to regulate "commerce with foreign nations, states and Indian Tribes."

At the same time, grassroots organizations of women began identifying all kinds of violence against women, including genital mutilation, dowry death, rape, forced sterilization, forced pregnancy, sex trafficking, honour deaths, as well as the custom of throwing acid into the face of a woman who had "dishonoured" her family.

Women's Human Rights

In 1995, Hillary Rodham Clinton famously declared, at the Beijing UN World Conference on Women, "If there is one message that echoes forth from this conference, let it be that human rights are women's rights and women's rights are human rights once and for all. Let us not forget that among those rights are the right to speak freely—and the right to be heard."

Americans have not greeted the twentieth anniversary of the VAWA with any significant fanfare. Even without any celebration, however, the legacy of VAWA remains influential.

Certainly, every Secretary-General of the United Nations heard her and felt obliged to speak against those customs that violated women's human rights. In 2006, Kofi Annan, wrote that "Violence against women and girls is a problem of pandemic proportions. At least one out of every three women around the world has been beaten, coerced into sex, or otherwise abused in her lifetime with the abuser usually someone known to her." Only last week Unicef published a major report, *Hidden in Plain Sight*, based on data in 190 countries, which revealed that 120 million girls and young women face serious sexual assault globally.

Eve Ensler, an American playwright who wrote the highly controversial and Tony-awarded play, "The Vagina Monologues," has tried to combat violence against women around the globe. Her play sought to teach women to value their bodies. She then renamed Valentine's Day, V-Day, to encourage women to speak out against the violence they faced. "I was obsessed with the statistic that 1 in 3 women on the planet will be raped or beaten in her lifetime," Ensler explained, "which is equal to over one billion women." And so she created One Billion Rising, which encourages men and women to break the "chain of violence" on V-Day by dancing in flash mobs against violence against women. The movement's web site functions like an international bulletin board, with posts from harassed female street artists in Cairo to a BBC program about the Yazidi women, a religious group that few people in the West had ever heard about before.

More than anything, war reinforces the custom that the victors get to rape the "spoils" of war. On June 19th, 2008, the United Nations Security Council declared such rape, when a tactic of war, to be a war crime against humanity. But that has changed little. Every day, in every war zone, we hear about women who have been abducted, kidnapped, and raped by their ethnic group's enemy. The truth is, millions of women are currently caught between murderous organisations like ISIS, which want to control every aspect of women's lives, and modern societies who have at least given lip service to the idea of gender equality.

The Need for Enforcement

So far, Americans have not greeted the twentieth anniversary of the VAWA with any significant fanfare. Even without any celebration, however, the legacy of VAWA remains influential. On August 30th, the nation's highest immigration court decided—for the first time—that a Guatemalan woman who had been a victim of severe domestic violence was eligible for asylum.

For years feminist immigration lawyers had failed to convince immigration courts that many women will die if they are deported and returned to their husbands. Such a change in American law is a perfect way to note the twentieth anniversary of VAWA, whose great achievement has been to change the terms of debate about violence against women.

Still, it is not new laws, but the enforcement of them that needs to be addressed. Violence against sex workers by customers and undocumented workers by employers, for example, is widespread, but these women fear reporting violence because of their illegal status. Domestic violence is just the tip of the iceberg. It may take another century before violence against women seems as barbaric and unacceptable as slavery does today.

Expansion of the Violence Against Women Act Is Fundamentally Flawed

David B. Muhlhausen and Christina Villegas

David B. Muhlhausen is a research fellow in empirical policy analysis at The Heritage Foundation and Christina Villegas is a visiting fellow at the Independent Women's Forum.

Certainly, domestic violence, especially against women, is deplorable. Violence against women—or anyone, for that matter—is rightfully a crime punishable by incarceration, depending on the degree of assault, in all 50 states and the District of Columbia.

The Violence Against Women Act

Despite the fact that the fight against domestic violence is waged mainly at the state and local levels, the federal government intervened during the Clinton Administration with the Violence Against Women Act (VAWA) of 1994. The Senate is now expected to consider the third reauthorization of the act—S. 1925. Unfortunately, S. 1925 includes radical and sweeping changes that greatly alter the original purpose and scope of the law, already problematic in its own right. For the reasons discussed below, there are very real substantive concerns about the expansion and misdirection of the new bill.

Instead of working to fix the bill's substantive problems, proponents of S. 1925 are attempting to characterize opponents of the bill as anti-woman and pro-domestic violence—an absurd proposition that stifles genuine debate on

David B. Muhlhausen and Christina Villegas, "Violence Against Women Act: Reauthorization Fundamentally Flawed," *Backgrounder*, no. 2673, Heritage Foundation, March 29, 2012. Copyright © 2012 The Heritage Foundation. All rights reserved. Reproduced with permission.

the legislation's many problems. Members of Congress should ignore the blatant mischaracterizations and give prudent consideration to the real effects of the VAWA and the consequences involved in its proposed reauthorization and expansion.

Although there is much work to be done to further reduce the incidence of domestic and family violence . . . the states and their subdivisions are to be commended for their adaptations and creative programs to address the scourge of domestic violence.

Specifically, Members of Congress should be concerned with the following flaws in S. 1925:

- The bill engages in mission creep by expanding VAWA to men and prisoners, despite the lack of scientifically rigorous evaluations to determine the effectiveness of existing VAWA programs;

- The bill expands upon the already duplicative grant programs authorized by VAWA; and

- Without precedent, the bill surrenders the rights of Americans who are not American Indians to racially exclusive tribal courts.

An Issue for the States

Under America's constitutional framework, police power is reserved to the states, and the states have laws to protect all citizens from crimes against them, including violence against women. The battle against domestic violence is thus waged and paid for, primarily, at the state and local levels.

Over the years, states and localities have adapted to the realities of domestic violence and have created specialized domestic violence courts, treatment programs, shelters, retraining programs, public awareness campaigns, prevention programs, and the like. State and local prosecutors, judges, and defense attorneys have taken specialized courses in the investigation, prosecution, treatment, and a constellation of other issues related to domestic violence, including violence against women.

Although there is much work to be done to further reduce the incidence of domestic and family violence—and it most likely will be an ongoing battle—the states and their subdivisions are to be commended for their adaptations and creative programs to address the scourge of domestic violence.

The VAWA initiated an extensive federal role in combating sex-based violence. Because proponents of the law argued that violence against women is a form of social control perpetuated by—according to their arguments—women's weaker social, political, and financial status, the substance of the VAWA focused largely on redistributing power and resources to female victims. This philosophy of group victimhood undermines equal protection and the rule of law and has been detrimental to the protection of victims generally.

Most modifications [of the VAWA] have nothing to do with women and have blurred the original intent of the law without necessarily improving its purpose or effectiveness.

To address the problem of domestic violence appropriately, the federal government should limit itself to handling tasks that have been assigned to it by the Constitution and which state and local governments cannot perform by themselves. The reflexive tendency to search for solutions at the national level is misguided and problematic. The problems faced by victims of domestic violence are serious, but they are almost entirely and inherently local in nature and should be addressed by state and local governments.

Thus, the original VAWA and its subsequent reauthorizations represent the federal government's overreach into matters more appropriately addressed by state and local governments.

A Departure from the Original Purpose

Violence against anybody is wrong, period. However, the radical and unnecessary changes proposed in S. 1925 would leave the law only tenuously connected to the VAWA's original purpose—reducing domestic violence against women.

Despite attempts to frame the debate over reauthorization solely in terms of women's rights, most modifications have nothing to do with women and have blurred the original intent of the law without necessarily improving its purpose or effectiveness.

For example, previous reauthorizations have expanded the VAWA to include services to young people and the elderly. Continuing VAWA's mission creep, S. 1925 fundamentally transforms the VAWA from a law originally specially focused on women to a law targeting both men and women.

Modifications in Services, Training, Officers, and Prosecutors Violence Against Women (STOP) grants are one example. S. 1925 alters the purpose areas of STOP grants to allow services to populations that previously have been denied access based on sexual orientation or gender identity.

An Inappropriate Expansion

In addition to this change, S. 1925 also contains a provision mandating that all VAWA grant programs not discriminate on the basis of gender identity and sexual orientation. S. 1925 includes an exception that allows sex segregation or sex-specific programming by VAWA grantees when such exclusions are deemed necessary. However, when such exclusions occur, grantees must provide comparable services to excluded individuals.

This requirement can place providers of services to domestic violence victims in difficult situations that run counter to their mission. Consider a program with limited resources that specializes in providing shelter to battered women. If passed, S. 1925 would require the shelter to provide comparable services to male victims of domestic violence. It may be entirely inappropriate for the shelter to have men share living areas, bedrooms, and bathrooms with women. Under this scenario, the shelter would have to find separate yet comparable accommodations. This requirement could create financial hardship for the shelter that exists to provide assistance specifically to female victims.

S. 1925 further widens the purpose areas of STOP grants to provide support services to victims of sexual violence in prison. Yet the overwhelming majority of these victims are male. This expansion is proposed in addition to, and in spite of, the Prison Rape Elimination Act of 2003, which authorizes grants specifically to address sexual violence in prisons.

By calling for a radical expansion of the VAWA, proponents of S. 1925 continue to expand the responsibilities of the Office of Violence Against Women (OVW), yet those duties are already duplicated by other federal agencies.

The Need to Validate Evidence of Effectiveness

The principal reasons for the existence of VAWA programs are to mitigate, reduce, or prevent the effects and occurrence of domestic violence. Despite being created in 1994, grant programs under the VAWA have not undergone large-scale, scientifically rigorous evaluations of effectiveness. The General Accounting Office concluded that previous evaluations of VAWA programs "demonstrated a variety of methodological limitations, raising concerns as to whether the evaluations will produce definitive results." Further, the evaluations were not representative of the types of programs funded nationally by the VAWA.

Nationally representative, scientifically rigorous impact evaluations should be used to determine whether these national grant programs actually produce their intended effects. Obviously, there is little merit in the continuation of programs that fail to ameliorate the social problems they target.

If Congress is intent on reauthorizing the VAWA, it should authorize funding for large-scale, multi-site experimental evaluations of VAWA grant programs. The Transitional Housing Assistance Grants are an ideal candidate for a large-scale experimental evaluation of effectiveness. Transitional housing programs typically operate at capacity and have a waiting list. When demand for services is greater than the supply of services, this situation is ideal for randomized experimentation. S. 1925 does not require scientifically rigorous evaluations of VAWA programs.

Duplication and Lack of Accountability

By calling for a radical expansion of the VAWA, proponents of S. 1925 continue to expand the responsibilities of the Office of Violence Against Women (OVW), yet those duties are already duplicated by other federal agencies. The proposed legislation creates new programs focused on children and the elderly.

For instance, S. 1925 creates a new grant program, Creating Hope Through Outreach, Options, Services, and Education for Children and Youth (CHOOSE Children and Youth), that provides services to young people up to age 24. The CHOOSE Children and Youth grants duplicate efforts by the Justice Department's Office of Juvenile Justice and Delinquency Prevention (OJJDP). OJJDP's Safe Start Initiative provides grants to prevent and diminish the effect of children's exposure to violence in their homes and communities. One of the primary problem areas on which these grants focus is the effect that domestic violence has on children, teens, and those in their early twenties.

The programs authorized by the VAWA duplicate programs offered by other federal agencies. The Justice Department's Office for Victims of Crime (OVC), for instance, has long considered domestic violence a priority funding area. OVC allocates a minimum of 10 percent of its grant funding made available under the Victims of Crime Act (VOCA) to programs that serve victims of domestic violence, sexual assault, and child abuse.

Numerous programs run by the Department of Health and Human Services provide domestic violence services as part of their missions. These programs include:

- Family Violence Prevention and Services/Grants for Battered Women's Shelters discretionary grants;

- Child Abuse and Neglect State Grants;

- The Healthy Start Initiative;

- The Family and Community Violence Prevention Program; and

- Community-Based Child Abuse Prevention Grants.

The United States Supreme Court ruled that Indian tribes, unless granted the power by Congress, do not have inherent jurisdiction to prosecute and punish non-Indians.

Surrendering Rights to Tribal Courts

American Indian tribes operate racially exclusive governments on their territories and lands. They have their own sovereign powers and operate separately from federal, state, and local governments under which all other Americans live. Additionally, American Indians operate and run their own tribal courts, which to date have limited jurisdiction. That jurisdiction is limited to members of Indian tribes.

One provision of S. 1925 would, for the first time in the nation's history, extend the criminal jurisdiction of tribal courts to people who are not members of an Indian tribe and who are accused of domestic violence that allegedly occurred on tribal territory. This surrender by federal or state governments of jurisdiction over Americans who are not members of Indian tribes is unprecedented, unnecessary, and dangerous.

Today, if John and Mary Smith were visiting a casino on an Indian reservation and John assaulted Mary, John would be charged by the federal government with assault and would be prosecuted by the local U.S. Attorney's Office in federal magistrate court. Under the radical proposal in S. 1925, John would be tried in one of several hundred different tribal courts.

This radical and unorthodox surrender of jurisdiction is particularly alarming because tribal courts do not necessarily adhere to the same constitutional provisions that protect the rights of all defendants in federal and state courts.

While S. 1925 mandates that tribal courts must grant defendants all the protections guaranteed by the United States Constitution, there appears to have been little study by the Senate Committee on the Judiciary of how capable tribal courts are in implementing this mandate. The committee did not even conduct a hearing on this issue while drafting the reauthorization legislation. This lack of legislative investigation is even more alarming since, in 1978, the United States Supreme Court ruled that Indian tribes, unless granted the power by Congress, do *not* have inherent jurisdiction to prosecute and punish non-Indians.

This proposal raises important issues that are worthy of further legislative investigation through hearings by the Senate Committee on the Judiciary.

A Federal Overreach

Fighting domestic violence is not, and never has been, a partisan issue. Everyone is against domestic violence. The law enforcement battle to combat domestic violence is (for the most part) waged and paid for by the state and local governments. Every state has statutes that punish domestic violence. Many jurisdictions have specialized courts that hold offenders accountable and offer services to victims. Court officers, including prosecutors, judges, and defense counsel, have attended specialized training to enable them to fully understand the unique challenges and dynamics posed by domestic violence and its interrelationship to other crimes, such as child abuse.

Using federal agencies and grant programs to fund the routine operations of domestic violence programs that state and local governments themselves could provide is a misuse of federal resources and a distraction from concerns that truly are the province of the federal government. Simply expanding this framework with extensive new provisions and programs that have been inadequately assessed is likely to facilitate waste, fraud, and abuse and will not better protect women or victims of violence generally.

In addition to federal overreach, the VAWA over the years has strayed from its original intent. The current reauthorization effort, S. 1925, is a gross distortion of the original law and is gravely flawed. [Editor's Note: The VAWA Reauthorization Act passed in 2013.]

The Violence Against Women Act Fails Because It Neglects Violence Against Men

Janice Shaw Crouse

Janice Shaw Crouse is senior fellow at Concerned Women for America's Beverly LaHaye Institute and author of the book Marriage Matters.

The Violence Against Women Act (VAWA) is up for reauthorization again this year [2012]. This newest version of VAWA—loaded up with even more leftist provisions—has hit a snag. First signed into law in 1994 with bipartisan support and reauthorized in 2000 and 2006, the legislation has become both a failure and a boondoggle, lining the pockets of feminist groups, vastly expanding federal, state and local bureaucracies, and becoming riddled with fraud.

Support for Reform

This year there are competing bills in the House (H.R. 4970) and Senate (S. 1925). In a climate of debt, deficit and government waste, the legitimate bone of contention is how best to reform the law, which has spawned dozens of failed programs. VAWA created a bureaucratic nightmare that targets the wrong women, those claiming nebulous "psychological harm," instead of actually helping battered women. In addition to not helping the women it is supposed to serve, VAWA has morphed into a rigid, inhumane law enforcement tool that hurts and denigrates men.

A national survey of registered voters introduced on July 17 by SAVE (Stop Abusive and Violent Environments), a non-

Janice Shaw Crouse, "Violence Against Women Act Needs Reform," *Washington Times*, July 24, 2012. Copyright © 2012 Washington Times. All rights reserved. Reproduced with permission.

profit victim-advocacy organization, shows that the majority of people surveyed agree it is time to reform VAWA. According to the results, domestic violence victims, younger people, Republicans and women are most likely to support VAWA reform. It found that 69.5 percent of those surveyed support reform to end waste and fraud, 65.9 percent support reform to stop discrimination, and 63.5 percent support reform to stop false allegations.

Victims of domestic violence or those who know a victim support reform even more, with 73 percent supporting reform to end waste and fraud and more than 68 percent supporting reform to stop discrimination and halt false allegations.

Statistics show there is not much difference between the rates of violence for men against women (6.4 percent) and women against men (6.3 percent).

The left has made much of the "war on women" Republicans supposedly are waging, in part by introducing and passing a VAWA bill in the GOP-dominated House instead of accepting the Senate version. However, more women surveyed seem to realize VAWA needs reform than men surveyed. More than 73 percent of women support reform to end waste and fraud compared to 70.6 percent of men; 71 percent of women support reform to stop discrimination compared to 66.6 percent of men; and 68.3 percent of women support reform to stop false allegations compared to 67.8 percent of men.

Discrimination Against Men

One of the key differences between the House and Senate bills is that the House bill is gender-neutral, protecting all Americans from domestic violence, while the Senate bill contains language that aims to protect specific groups, including homosexual and transgender Americans. The House language takes an important step toward reforming a law that has created a climate of suspicion against men and a situation in which men are arrested on flimsy excuses, while women have their legal fees paid, enabling them to get a divorce and keep a man out of his house and away from his children. An accused man is often fired from his job, alienated from his friends and community, and assumed guilty until somehow he is able to prove he is innocent.

Statistics show there is not much difference between the rates of violence for men against women (6.4 percent) and women against men (6.3 percent). Robert Franklin, a Texas lawyer who is on the board of Fathers and Families, listed some enlightening statistics in a recent article that point to the need for the law to cover all victims of domestic violence because men are victims, too:

- 35 percent of victims of severe domestic violence are men but only 1 percent of federal funds goes to assist them.

- A study of students at two universities showed that 29 percent of women and 22 percent of men admitted to physically assaulting a date.

- A University of New Hampshire study on dating violence in 32 countries showed women were the aggressors more often than men.

- The Liz Claiborne Institute found in its Teen Relationship Abuse Survey that 17 percent of boys and 13 percent of girls had been hit, slapped or pushed by a dating partner.

- A 2009 Centers for Disease Control study showed that when there was reciprocal violence in a domestic relationship, it was women who hit first 70 percent of the time and then men responded with violence.

The original VAWA was based on good intentions, but as with most things that originate in Washington, the result over the years has been to create an enormous bureaucracy that runs amok with fraud, lacks appropriate oversight, contains no means of accountability and consists of many duplicate programs providing the same assistance to the same groups of people. President [Barack] Obama has said he would veto H.R. 4970 but supports S. 1925. Unless this law is reformed (and H.R. 4970 takes steps to do so) it will continue to discriminate against men, underserve actual victims of violence and provide millions of taxpayer dollars to build radical feminist power structures instead of ending intimate partner violence. [Editor's Note: Neither bill mentioned here passed, but the VAWA Reauthorization Act was passed in 2013.]

CHAPTER 4

What Is the Extent of Violence Against Women Worldwide?

Overview: Violence Against Women Worldwide

United Nations

The United Nations is an intergovernmental organization that aims to promote peace, security, human rights, and development around the globe.

According to a 2013 global review of available data, 35 per cent of women worldwide have experienced either physical and/or sexual intimate partner violence or non-partner sexual violence. However, some national violence studies show that up to 70 per cent of women have experienced physical and/or sexual violence in their lifetime from an intimate partner.

Violence Against Women Worldwide

It is estimated that of all women killed in 2012, almost half were killed by intimate partners or family members.

More often than not, cases of violence against women go unreported. For instance, a study based on interviews with 42,000 women across the 28 Member States of the European Union revealed that only 14 per cent of women reported their most serious incident of intimate partner violence to the police, and 13 per cent reported their most serious incident of non-partner violence to the police.

Worldwide, more than 700 million women alive today were married as children (below 18 years of age). More than one in three—or some 250 million—were married before 15. Child brides are often unable to effectively negotiate safer sex, leaving themselves vulnerable to sexually transmitted infections, including HIV, along with early pregnancy. The fact that

United Nations, "Facts and Figures: Ending Violence Against Women," October 2014. Copyright © 2014 UN Women. All rights reserved. Reproduced with permission.

girls are not physically mature enough to give birth, places both mothers and their babies at risk. Poor girls are also 2.5 times more likely to marry in childhood than those living in the wealthiest quintile.

Women and girls represent 55 per cent of the estimated 20.9 million victims of forced labour worldwide, and 98 per cent of the estimated 4.5 million forced into sexual exploitation.

Among ever-married girls, current and/or former intimate partners are the most commonly reported perpetrators of physical violence in all the countries with available data.

Around 120 million girls worldwide (slightly more than 1 in 10) have experienced forced intercourse or other forced sexual acts at some point in their lives.

More than 133 million girls and women have experienced some form of female genital mutilation (FGM) in the 29 countries in Africa and the Middle East where the harmful practice is most common. Beyond extreme physical and psychological pain, girls who undergo FGM are at risk of prolonged bleeding, infection (including HIV), infertility, complications during pregnancy and death.

Trafficking ensnares millions of women and girls in modern-day slavery. Women and girls represent 55 per cent of the estimated 20.9 million victims of forced labour worldwide, and 98 per cent of the estimated 4.5 million forced into sexual exploitation.

Between 40 and 50 per cent of women in European Union countries experience unwanted sexual advances, physical contact or other forms of sexual harassment at work.

In the United States, 83 per cent of girls in grades 8 through 11 (aged 12 to 16) have experienced some form of sexual harassment in public schools.

Extra Vulnerabilities for Violence

Women in urban areas are twice as likely as men to experience violence, particularly in developing countries.

In New Delhi, a 2010 study found that 66 per cent of women reported experiencing sexual harassment between two and five times during the past year.

Research conducted in different countries has documented associations between HIV and physical and/or sexual violence, both as a risk factor for HIV infection and as a potential consequence of being identified as living with HIV. A decade of cross-sectional research from African countries, including Rwanda, Tanzania, South Africa and more recently, India, has consistently found women who have experienced partner violence to be more likely to be infected with HIV.

In the United States, 11.8 per cent of new HIV infections among women more than 20 years old during the previous year were attributed to intimate partner violence.

The High Cost of Violence

Annual costs of intimate partner violence have been calculated at USD 5.8 billion in the United States in 2003 and GBP 22.9 billion in England and Wales in 2004.

A 2009 study in Australia estimated the cost of violence against women and children at AUD 13.6 billion per year.

A recent estimation of the costs of domestic violence against women at the household level to the economy in Viet Nam suggests that both out-of-pocket expenditures and lost earnings represent nearly 1.4 per cent of GDP in that country. An estimate of overall productivity loss, however, comes to 1.8 per cent of GDP.

War's Overlooked Victims

The Economist

The Economist *is a global magazine of news, analysis, and opinion.*

Shortly after the birth of her sixth child, Mathilde went with her baby into the fields to collect the harvest. She saw two men approaching, wearing what she says was the uniform of the FDLR, a Rwandan militia. Fleeing them she ran into another man, who beat her head with a metal bar. She fell to the ground with her baby and lay still. Perhaps thinking he had murdered her, the man went away. The other two came and raped her, then they left her for dead.

Mathilde's story is all too common. Rape in war is as old as war itself. After the sack of Rome 16 centuries ago Saint Augustine called rape in wartime an "ancient and customary evil." For soldiers, it has long been considered one of the spoils of war. Antony Beevor, a historian who has written about rape during the Soviet conquest of Germany in 1945, says that rape has occurred in war since ancient times, often perpetrated by indisciplined soldiers. But he argues that there are also examples in history of rape being used strategically, to humiliate and to terrorise, such as the Moroccan *regulares* in Spain's civil war.

As the reporting of rape has improved, the scale of the crime has become more horrifyingly apparent. And with the Bosnian war of the 1990s came the widespread recognition that rape has been used systematically as a weapon of war and that it must be punished as an egregious crime. In 2008 the UN Security Council officially acknowledged that rape has been used as a tool of war. With these kinds of resolutions

The Economist, "War's Overlooked Victims," January 13, 2011. Copyright © 2011 The Economist. All rights reserved. Reproduced with permission.

and global campaigns against rape in war, the world has become more sensitive. At least in theory, the Geneva Conventions, governing the treatment of civilians in war, are respected by politicians and generals in most decent states. Generals from rich countries know that their treatment of civilians in the theatre of war comes under ever closer scrutiny. The laws and customs of war are clear. But in many parts of the world, in the Hobbesian anarchy of irregular war, with ill-disciplined private armies or militias, these norms carry little weight.

Many [rape] victims are killed by their assailants. Others die of injuries. Many do not report rape because of the stigma.

Take Congo; it highlights both how horribly common rape is, and how hard it is to document and measure, let alone stop. The eastern part of the country has been a seething mess since the Rwandan genocide of 1994. In 2008 the International Rescue Committee (IRC), a humanitarian group, estimated that 5.4m people had died in "Africa's world war." Despite peace deals in 2003 and 2008, the tempest of violence has yet fully to subside. As Congo's army and myriad militias do battle, the civilians suffer most. Rape has become an ugly and defining feature of the conflict.

Plenty of figures on how many women have been raped are available but none is conclusive. In October Roger Meece, the head of the United Nations in Congo, told the UN Security Council that 15,000 women had been raped throughout the country in 2009 (men suffer too, but most victims are female). The UN Population Fund estimated 17,500 victims for the same period. The IRC says it treated 40,000 survivors in the eastern province of South Kivu alone between 2003 and 2008.

"The data only tell you so much," says Hillary Margolis, who runs the IRC's sexual-violence programme in North Kivu. These numbers are the bare minimum; the true figures may be much higher. Sofia Candeias, who co-ordinates the UN Development Programme's Access to Justice project in Congo, points out that more rapes are reported in places with health services. In the areas where fighting is fiercest, women may have to walk hundreds of miles to find anyone to tell that they have been attacked. Even if they can do so, it may be months or years after the assault. Many victims are killed by their assailants. Others die of injuries. Many do not report rape because of the stigma.

Congo's horrors are mind-boggling. A recent study by the Harvard Humanitarian Initiative and Oxfam examined rape survivors at the Panzi Hospital in Bukavu, a town in South Kivu province. Their ages ranged from three to 80. Some were single, some married, some widows. They came from all ethnicities. They were raped in homes, fields and forests. They were raped in front of husbands and children. Almost 60% were gang-raped. Sons were forced to rape mothers, and killed if they refused.

The attention paid to Congo reflects growing concern about rape in war. Historically the taboo surrounding rape has been so strong that few cases were reported; evidence of wartime rape before the 20th century is scarce. With better reporting, the world has woken up to the scale of the crime. The range of sexual violence in war has become apparent: the abduction of women as sex slaves, sexualised torture and mutilation, rape in public or private.

In some wars all parties engage in it. In others it is inflicted mainly by one side. Rape in wars in Africa has had a lot of attention in recent years, but it is not just an African problem. Conflicts with high levels of rape between 1980 and 2009 were most numerous in sub-Saharan Africa, according to Dara Kay Cohen of the University of Minnesota. But only a third of sub-Saharan Africa's 28 civil wars saw the worst levels of rape—compared with half of Eastern Europe's nine. And no part of the world has escaped the scourge.

You can rape to terrorise people or force them to leave an area . . . but rape is not effective when you want long-term, reliable intelligence from them or to rule them in the future.

The anarchy and impunity of war goes some way to explaining the violence. The conditions of war are often conducive to rape. Young, ill-trained men, fighting far from home, are freed from social and religious constraints. The costs of rape are lower, the potential rewards higher. And for ill-fed, underpaid combatants, rape can be a kind of payment.

Widespread, but Not Inevitable

Then consider the type of wars fought today. Many recent conflicts have involved not organised armies but scrappy militias fighting amid civilians. As wars have moved from battle-fields to villages, women and girls have become more vulnerable. For many, the home front no longer exists; every house is now on the front line.

But rape in war is not inevitable. In El Salvador's civil war, it was rare. When it did occur it was almost always carried out by state forces. The left-wing militias fighting against the government for years relied on civilians for information. You can rape to terrorise people or force them to leave an area, says Elisabeth Wood, a professor at Yale University and the Santa Fe Institute, but rape is not effective when you want long-term, reliable intelligence from them or to rule them in the future.

Some groups commit all kinds of other atrocities, but abhor rape. The absence of sexual violence in the Tamil Tigers' forced displacement of tens of thousands of Muslims from the

Jaffna peninsula in 1990 is a case in point. Rape is often part of ethnic cleansing but it was strikingly absent here. Tamil mores prohibit sex between people who are not married and sex across castes (though they are less bothered about marital rape). What is more, Ms Wood explains, the organisation's strict internal discipline meant commanders could enforce these judgments.

Some leaders, such as Jean-Pierre Bemba, a Congolese militia boss who is now on trial for war-crimes in The Hague, say they lack full control over their troops. But a commander with enough control to direct soldiers in military operations can probably stop them raping, says Ms Wood. A decision to turn a blind eye may have less to do with lack of control, and more with a chilling assessment of rape's use as a terror tactic.

Rape is a means of subduing foes and civilians without having to engage in the risky business of battle. Faced with rape, civilians flee, leaving their land and property to their attackers. In August rebel militias raped around 240 people over four days in the Walikale district of eastern Congo. The motives for the attack are unclear. The violence may have been to intimidate the population into providing the militia with gold and tin from nearby mines. Or maybe one bit of the army was colluding with the rebels to avoid being replaced by another bit and losing control of the area and its resources. In Walikale, at least, rape seems to have been a deliberate tactic, not a random one, says Ms Margolis.

[In Rwanda,] Hutu propaganda may not have openly called for rape, but it certainly suggested that the Hutu cause would be well served by the sexual violation of Tutsi women.

At worst, rape is a tool of ethnic cleansing and genocide, as in Bosnia, Darfur and Rwanda. Rape was first properly recognised as a weapon of war after the conflict in Bosnia.

Though all sides were guilty, most victims were Bosnian Muslims assaulted by Serbs. Muslim women were herded into "rape camps" where they were raped repeatedly, usually by groups of men. The full horrors of these camps emerged in hearings at the war-crimes tribunal on ex-Yugoslavia in The Hague; victims gave evidence in writing or anonymously. After the war some perpetrators said that they had been ordered to rape—either to ensure that non-Serbs would flee certain areas, or to impregnate women so that they bore Serb children. In 1995, when Croatian forces over-ran Serb-held areas, there were well-attested cases of sexual violence against both women and men.

In the Sudanese region of Darfur, rape and other forms of sexual violence have also been a brutally effective way to terrorise and control civilians. Women are raped in and around the refugee camps that litter the region, mostly when they leave the camps to collect firewood, water and food. Those of the same ethnicity as the two main rebel groups have been targeted most as part of the campaign of ethnic cleansing. According to Human Rights Watch, rape is chronically underreported, partially because in the mostly Muslim region sexual violence is a sensitive subject. Between October 2004 and February 2005 Médecins Sans Frontières, a French charity, treated almost 500 women and girls in South Darfur. The actual number of victims is likely to be much higher.

Tacit Approval

In the Rwandan genocide rape was "the rule and its absence the exception," in the words of the UN. In the weeks before the killings began, Hutu-controlled newspapers ran cartoons showing Tutsi women having sex with Belgian peacekeepers, who were seen as allies of Paul Kagame's Rwandan Patriotic Front. Inger Skjelsbaek, deputy director of the Peace Research Institute in Oslo, argues that Hutu propaganda may not have openly called for rape, but it certainly suggested that the Hutu cause would be well served by the sexual violation of Tutsi women. Jens Meierhenrich, a Rwanda-watcher at the London School of Economics, says that even if high-level commanders did not tell men to rape, they gave tacit approval. Lower-ranking officers may have openly encouraged the crime.

Out of Rwanda's horror came the first legal verdict that acknowledged rape as part of a genocidal campaign. After the conviction of Jean Paul Akayesu, a local politician, the International Criminal Tribunal for Rwanda said systematic sexual violence, perpetrated against Tutsi women and them alone, had been an integral part of the effort to wipe out the Tutsis.

For combatants who know little about each other, complicity in rape can serve as a bond. The Revolutionary United Front (RUF) in Sierra Leone, most of whose members say they were kidnapped into its ranks and then raped thousands during the civil war, is a case in point. Ms Cohen argues that armed groups that are not socially cohesive, particularly those whose fighters have been forcibly recruited, are more likely to commit rape, especially gang rape, so as to build internal ties.

There is little prospect of justice for the victims of rape.

For the victims and their families, rape does the opposite. The shame and degradation of rape rip apart social bonds. In societies where a family's honour rests on the sexual purity of its women, the blame for the loss of that honour often falls not upon the rapist, but the raped. In Bangladesh, where most of the victims were Muslim, the use of rape was not only humiliating for them as individuals but for their families and communities. The then prime minister, Mujibur Rahman, tried to counter this by calling them heroines who needed protection and reintegration. Some men agreed but most did not; they demanded sweeteners in the form of extra dowry payments from the authorities.

In Congo, despite the efforts of activists, rape still brings shame to the victim, says Ms Margolis: "People can sit around and talk about the importance of removing the stigma in the abstract, but when it comes to their own wives or daughters or sisters, it is a different story." Many are rejected by their family and stigmatised by their community after being raped.

There is little prospect of justice for the victims of rape. Mr Akayesu is one of the few people brought to book for rape in war. Though wartime rape is prohibited under the Geneva rules, sexual violence has often been prosecuted less fiercely than other war crimes. But the Balkan war-crimes court broke new ground by issuing verdicts treating rape as a crime against humanity. The convictions of three men for the rape, torture and sexual enslavement of women in the Bosnian town of Foca was a big landmark.

But in Congo the court system is in pieces. There have been fewer than 20 prosecutions of rape as either a war crime or a crime against humanity. The American Bar Association, which helps victims bring their cases to court in eastern Congo, has processed around 145 cases in the past two years. This has resulted in about 45 trials and 36 convictions based on domestic legislation, including a law introduced in 2006 to try and address the problem of sexual violence. Those who work with the survivors of rape in Congo have mixed feelings about the 2006 law. It has pricked consciences and made people more aware of their rights, concedes Ms Margolis. It creates a theoretical accountability that could help punish perpetrators. But for women seeking justice, it has yet to have much impact. "There is still a glimmer of hope in people's eyes when they talk about the law. But the judicial and security systems need to be improved so that it can be applied better, or people may lose confidence in it," Ms Margolis says.

Huge practical problems beset the legal system in Congo, says Richard Malengule, head of the Gender and Justice programme at HEAL Africa, a hospital in Goma. People have to walk 300km to get to a court. There is no money and no training for the police. Even if people are arrested, they are often released within a few days, in many cases by making a deal with the victim's family or the court. Those that go to jail often escape within days. Many prisons have no door—or corrupt guards.

Enduring Effects

Given the parlous state of Congo's judiciary, raising the number of prosecutions may not help. Some want more international involvement. Justine Masika, who runs an organisation in Goma seeking justice for the victims of sex crimes, says Congolese courts must work with international ones in prosecuting rape. But "hybrid" courts require some commitment from the local government; Congo's rulers do not show much commitment to tackling rape. The International Criminal Court is investigating crimes, including rape, in Congo but gathering necessary evidence is hard.

Even when wars end, rape continues. Humanitarian agencies in Congo report high levels of rape in areas that are quite peaceful now.

Raising global awareness is another avenue; it helps lessen the stigma. Various UN resolutions over the past ten years have highlighted and condemned sexual violence against women and girls and called on countries to do more to combat it. But worthy language will not be enough.

Worse, the UN has faced criticism for failing to protect Congolese civilians from rape. In the Walikale attack, one UN official worries that the body is not meeting its obligations to protect civilians. He accepts that in remote places it is hard for peacekeepers to reach civilians, but insists that this does not justify the UN's failure in Walikale. He is dubious, too, about the investigations into the incident. "All these interviews, these investigations, what have they achieved? The survivors are in-terviewed again and again and again? Where does that get them?"

Without the presence of the UN, atrocities would be even more widespread, says Mr Malengule. But in the long term, he says, more pressure must be put on Congo's government to tackle rape. At present, one aid worker laments, it just gets a lot of lip-service. The government would rather Congo were not known as the world's rape capital, but it shows little inter-est in real change.

Even when wars end, rape continues. Humanitarian agen-cies in Congo report high levels of rape in areas that are quite peaceful now. Again, it is hard to assess numbers. Figures for rape before the war do not exist. A greater willingness to re-port rape may account for the apparent increase. But years of fighting have resulted in a culture of rape and violence, says Mr Malengule. Efforts to reintegrate ex-combatants into soci-ety have been short and unsuccessful, with little follow-up to assess results. Add to that the dismal judicial system, and the outlook is grim.

It is bleaker still when you see how long rape's effects en-dure. Rebels seized Angelique's village in 1994. They slit her husband's throat. Then they bound her between two trees, arms and legs tied apart. Seven men raped her before she fainted. She does not know how many raped her after that. Then they shoved sticks in her vagina. Tissue between her va-gina and rectum was ripped, and she developed a fistula. For 16 years she leaked urine and faeces. Now she is getting medi-cal treatment, but justice is a distant dream.

Violence Against Women in Latin America: Is It Getting Worse?

Sara Miller Llana and Sibylla Brodzinsky

Sara Miller Llana is a staff writer for The Christian Science Monitor *and Sibylla Brodzinsky is an independent foreign correspondent.*

Like the majority of women in Colombia, Viviana Hernandez won't leave her house without makeup. She applies a thick layer of foundation and outlines her slightly deformed lips with red liner. She draws in her eyebrows—she lost her natural ones—and hides the few lashes she has left and her disfigured eyes behind the large dark sunglasses that she's worn day and night since an attacker threw acid on her face five years ago.

Ms. Hernandez has no doubt it was her estranged partner who ordered the attack. Once she came out of intensive care at the hospital, she remembers him calling her cellphone, telling her that no one else would want her now but him.

Hernandez's is but one face of violence against women in Latin America, a worrying trend in a region that has seen enormous advances for women over the past decade. Forty percent of the region is now led by women: There are female heads of state in Brazil, Argentina, Costa Rica, Trinidad and Tobago, and Jamaica. Women have reached equal access to education and have increasingly joined the workforce. Awareness has also grown around the issues of violence against women through a spate of legislation aimed at protecting them.

Sara Miller Llana and Sibylla Brodzinsky, "Violence Against Women in Latin America: Is It Getting Worse?," *Christian Science Monitor*, November 20, 2012. Copyright © 2012 Christian Science Monitor. All rights reserved. Reproduced with permission.

But this progress stands in sharp contrast to gender-based violence that has long plagued the region, and is now manifesting itself in new and dangerous ways.

Violence against women is linked to a number of factors, including hard economic times and communities where violent crime is endemic.

In some countries violence against women is far worse today, from a spike in femicides—the gender-based killing of women—in places like El Salvador and Honduras, where the drug war has become deadlier, to the disturbing trend of acid attacks against women in Colombia. In light of the Nov. 25 United Nations International Day for the Elimination of Violence Against Women, this uptick leaves many questioning what can be done.

Why Target Women?

Last April Nadine Gasman, the head of UNiTE to End Violence against Women for Latin America and the Caribbean, a UN initiative that fights impunity and works to change cultural attitudes, attended a meeting with police, prosecutors, and justice ministries across the region to talk about violence against women.

"What was clear is that there is an increased number of [acts of] exacerbated cruelty," Ms. Gasman says. "We don't understand why."

Violence against women is linked to a number of factors, including hard economic times and communities where violent crime is endemic. But Gasman, like many observers, says that part of the spike in several countries could be attributed to different paces of change in society: Women are reporting crime more, but justice systems are not responding, making them even more vulnerable.

"Women are asking for rights, and men get very violent; and because the system is so cumbersome and does not provide responses quickly enough, violence gets worse and worse," Gasman says.

Femicides in Mexico, Guatemala, Honduras, and El Salvador have all shot up in recent years, registering some of the highest rates in the world. The latter has seen the biggest spike in femicide in Latin America, with 637 women murdered in 2011, almost quadruple the rate from a decade ago, says Silvia Juarez, who heads the violence against women program for the Organization of Salvadoran Women for Peace.

In 2009, Mexico recorded its highest number of femicides since 1985, recording 1,858 deaths, according to a UN report.

"We have documented an alarming growth of femicide in the country," says Jose Martinez Cruz, the head of a human rights organization in the state of Morelos in central Mexico.

Patsili Toledo, a Chilean lawyer active in women's rights issues, says the drug war, like most armed conflict, is particularly dangerous for women. They become more vulnerable amid a breakdown of law and order and social mores.

Gender violence is still firmly entrenched in Latin America. This is especially true in terms of domestic violence, which in some places is getting worse and more brutal.

Women have certainly become victims of the drug trade as they participate in it; but in some cases, women are used as a form of social cohesion among gang members. The men can bond over inflicting violence against women. That may have been a motive in another setback for women in Mexico, when a group of teens on a spiritual retreat in July was overtaken by a gang that raped five women and girls.

Three of the suspects admitted to doing so after other gang members pressured them.

"The bodies of these women are a way of hurting the enemy," Ms. Toledo says. "There are also many, many more guns and weapons. That [kind of] domestic environment is more dangerous for everyone."

But beyond the context of organized crime, gender violence is still firmly entrenched in Latin America. This is especially true in terms of domestic violence, which in some places is getting worse and more brutal.

The number of femicides in Chile, which defines it as the murder of a woman by a current or former partner or husband, has jumped 31 percent in the first half of 2012 compared with the same period last year, according to a study by the nongovernmental group Activa and Pedro de Valdivia University.

'Permanent face of Violence'

At least 282 women were murdered in gender-related crime in 2011 in Argentina; and among 542 women killed there in the past two years, 43 died after being set on fire by their attackers, according to La Casa del Encuentro, a women's rights organization in Buenos Aires.

In Colombia, a phenomenon of acid attacks against women has been reported. It is the only country in the Western Hemisphere to record such acts, which are more common in places like Bangladesh and Pakistan.

"Acid attack victims are the most visible and permanent face of violence against women," says Linda Guerrero, a plastic surgeon who heads a foundation for burn victims in Bogotá and spearheads a campaign to highlight the prevalence of such attacks in Colombia.

In 2011, official records show 42 women in Colombia were attacked with acid, and in 2012 there have been at least 19. But Olga Victoria Rubio, a city councilwoman in Bogotá, says the number is much higher than what the official records show.

"Most women are attacked by their partners and are terrified of reporting it," Ms. Rubio says.

In Hernandez's case, her attack is not included in any official registry as an acid attack. Though she reported the event, no investigation was ever opened, she says, because prosecutors left it up to her to collect evidence.

Additionally, many victims see little point in reporting the attacks because they are treated as misdemeanors, and perpetrators are not likely to face harsh repercussions, Rubio says. A bill making its way through Colombia's Congress would change that, classifying acid attacks as attempted homicide.

A Silver Lining?

The numbers are shocking but reflect some positive news: More women are reporting the crime, and the news media are paying attention to it, particularly when it comes to domestic violence.

A 2010 law in El Salvador and one in 2008 in Guatemala seek stronger protections for female victims of violence.

"For a long time, women didn't come forward," says Alessandra Guedes, the regional adviser on intrafamily violence at the Pan American Health Organization, the regional office of the World Health Organization, and coauthor of a forthcoming study comparing violence against women in 12 countries in the region. "It was very much a private issue . . . dealt [with] within four walls."

Initiatives such as all-female police stations in Brazil for battered women have made it easier for women to come forward. Nonprofit organizations are reaching out to young men and boys to help chip away at machismo. There is also a spate of new legislation across the region.

A 2010 law in El Salvador and one in 2008 in Guatemala seek stronger protections for female victims of violence. On Nov. 15 the Argentine congress passed a law making femicide a crime that carries a life sentence.

In Colombia, new legislation that went into effect this summer stipulates that victims of domestic violence cannot withdraw their complaints and that persons other than the victim can report violence. Medical personnel who suspect a person is the victim of domestic violence are now obligated to report their suspicions to police.

Another initiative seeks to include femicide in the Colombian penal code, a bill that was prompted by a brutal attack on Rosa Elvira Cely in a Bogotá park last May. Ms. Cely, a single mother who sold candy on the streets, was found under a tree; she was barely alive after being raped and tortured. She died four days later. The brutality of her attack prompted nationwide demonstrations and campaigns.

"We had been working on drafting something like this for some time, but what happened to Rosa Elvira was the last straw. It mobilized so many people," says Teresa Martinez, an aide to Sen. Gloria Inés Ramirez, who is sponsoring Colombia's bill.

The 'Biggest Challenge'

But women's rights advocates say that impunity is their biggest challenge, which is one of the main priorities of the UNiTE campaign. According to the Inter-American Commission on Human Rights, half of all Central American women have been subjected to violence during their adult lives, but half of all verdicts delivered in cases of violence against women end in acquittals.

"Impunity sends a message of tolerance. I can rape you and nothing happens, and I can kill you because nothing will happen," says Ms. Juarez from El Salvador.

The limits of legislation are clear in Brazil. In 2006, the Maria da Penha Law was signed, increasing the maximum sentences for domestic violence from one year to three, and providing protective measures for at-risk women. The year following its enactment the number of women murdered dropped significantly.

But according to a 2012 study by the Institute Sangari, by 2008 the rate had returned to pre-law levels.

In February, a congressional investigative committee in Brazil began analyzing cases in which public officials have refused to invoke the law.

Sen. Ana Rita, a member of the committee, says the law faces resistance from judges. She cites the recent case of Renata Rocha Araújo, a 28-year-old who was turned down twice for protective measures against her husband by a judge who argued that the María da Penha Law was not made to break up families. She was killed in May.

Senator Rita implored the nation to demand more from all parts of society.

"What vision of family do these judges have that they ignore the violence against women in their homes?" she says.

Why India Is Sitting on a Social Time-Bomb of Violence Against Women

Sunny Hundal

Sunny Hundal is editor of the political blog Liberal Conspiracy.

Imagine a world where the proportion of girls being born is so low that large proportions of males just cannot find partners when they come of age. In such a world they are more likely to congregate in gangs for company. In turn, that means they are more likely to engage in risky behaviour: i.e. commit crime, do drugs and engage in violence against women. In gangs, men are more likely to harass women and even commit rape.

But this isn't some dystopian fantasy—there are 37 million more men than women in India, and most of them are of marriageable age given the relatively young population. A social time-bomb is now setting off there with terrifying consequences.

While researching for my e-book on violence against women in India, earlier this year I came across an extraordinary article on why some brothers living in the same household were sharing a wife rather than marrying separate women.

Let that sink in for a moment. The *Times of India* reported in 2005 on instances where between two and five brothers living in a house, in rural areas in the state of Punjab, had married the same woman. It was extraordinary not just for what was in it, but for what was left out.

Sunny Hundal, "Why India Is Sitting on a Social Time-Bomb of Violence Against Women," *New Statesman* (UK), December 16, 2013. Copyright © 2013 New Statesman. All rights reserved. Reproduced with permission.

The article—"Draupadis bloom in rural Punjab"—cited two reasons for these polyandric arrangements: they prevented the household from splitting into multiple families and therefore dividing the meagre land they owned; men just could not find wives to settle down with. [The women are called "Draupadis" in reference to the princess who married five brothers in the Hindu epic *The Mahabharata*]. Punjabi writer Gurdial Singh told the *Times of India*: "the small landholdings and skewed sex ratio have abetted the problem."

Not enough people inside India and outside realise the problem there is on a different scale because of the scale of sex-selection, which has meant that millions of girls who should be in the population are systematically wiped out.

A year ago, after the atrocious and widely-publicised gang-rape and murder of the student in Delhi, there has been much discussion of what is going on in India. Of course, the epidemic of violence against women is not an Indian problem alone.

But something more is going on there that deserves special attention. Not enough people inside India and outside realise the problem there is on a different scale because of the scale of sex-selection, which has meant that millions of girls who should be in the population are systematically wiped out.

We can put a number on this. To have a natural sex ratio like most of the world, India would need more women than men in its population. Around 23 million more women in fact. So, adding the 37 million (to equalise the number of men and women) to 23 million gives us an approximate figure of 60 million women "missing" from the population of India.

Punjab is ground-zero for this phenomena. Dividing up small land-holdings are not a new issue for the agricultural state; it's the skewed sex-ratio which is the real problem. In a report published in 2009, the charity Action Aid India found that among some communities in Punjab there were as less as 300 girls per 1,000 boys. Overall, it is among the worst states in the country for the female to male ratio.

There's a huge deficit of women because families fear the cost of raising a daughter. It is a commonly practiced tradition (despite being outlawed) that the bride's family pays a large sum of money to the groom's family at the wedding. Plus, women are generally not seen as bread-winners and or allowed to inherit wealth like men in some states.

In the 1980s, an infamous ad run by private hospitals stated: "Pay 5,000 rupees today [to have an abortion] and save 50,000 rupees [in dowry payments] tomorrow." It was soon banned but the sentiments linger on. Sex-selection is now spreading to rural areas as the technology gets cheaper and enforcement of the law remains ineffectual. Media exposes of doctors providing sex-selection services and offering to abort girls are commonplace, but they have little overall impact because demand is too strong.

But sex-selection doesn't paint the full picture. Large proportions of women are missing also because many poor families simply murder girl infants at birth if they can't afford ultrasound and abortion services. Others simply neglect girls as they're growing up (India is far and away the world's worst for differences in gender for child mortality). In fact, the sex-ratio of girls to boys under the age of 6 keeps dropping.

What's extraordinary about all this is that until the gang-rape last year, the media paid very little attention to such issues. The *Times of India* report I mentioned for example neglected to interview any women and ask if they were happy with their arrangement. Neither does the reporter look into how widespread these arrangements were and what impact they were having on communities. It's as if they were reporting on the price of onions, with a positive gloss of such marriages are 'blooming'.

In reality, there are increasing stories of women being kidnapped or trafficked to be forced into marriages because men cannot find brides. Yet, until recently, there was an extraordinary unwillingness in the media to join the dots. The gang-rape last year started a debate about violence against women in India, but for many women the impact of this social time-bomb are being felt now.

Surging Violence Against Women in Iraq

Zahra Radwan and Zoe Blumenfeld

Zahra Radwan is the program officer for Middle East & North Africa at Global Fund for Women and Zoe Blumenfeld is the communications manager at Global Fund for Women.

Shortly after their conquest of Mosul, young men armed with assault rifles went door to door in Iraq's second-largest city, taking "women who are not owned" for *jihad al-nikah*, or sex jihad.

From June 9–12, women's rights activists documented 13 cases of women who were kidnapped and raped by militants of the Islamic State of Iraq and Syria (ISIS) or DAIISH, the Arabic shorthand for the group's name. Of the 13 women, four of them committed suicide because they couldn't stand the shame. One woman's brother committed suicide because he could not bear the fact that he was unable to protect his sister.

The dispatches from Mosul are just one account of the extreme violence that has plagued Iraq since Sunni ISIS militants seized control over large portions of the country. Being a woman in Iraq was difficult before the current conflict. But the current wave of militarization threatens to make life even worse.

"Women are being taken in broad daylight," said Yanar Mohammad, co-founder and president of the Organization of Women's Freedom in Iraq, a Global Fund for Women grantee partner. "Men have the weapons to do whatever they want and [ISIS'] way of dealing with things is to kill."

Zahra Radwan and Zoe Blumenfeld, "Surging Violence Against Women in Iraq," *Foreign Policy in Focus*, June 26, 2014. Copyright © 2014 Foreign Policy in Focus. All rights reserved. Reproduced with permission.

Now military leaders are handing guns to young, untrained, undereducated, and unemployed Shia men. These men are promised big salaries if they leave their homes to fight, according to an anonymous Global Fund ally in Baghdad.

The sectarian conflict [in Iraq] has forced most women's rights organizations to scale back their programs.

"When we [women] commute to our office, walk in the street, or take the bus, we experience harassment," added the Global Fund ally, who remains anonymous due to security concerns. "But now, all of the men have weapons. I think maybe he will kidnap or shoot me if I don't do what he wants. They will shoot and do anything, and because of the fatwa [urging able-bodied Iraqis to take up arms against Sunni extremists] no one asks questions."

Sectarian Violence Slows Women's Progress

With a death toll of 1,000 and rising since the beginning of June, the sectarian conflict has forced most women's rights organizations to scale back their programs.

The Organization of Women's Freedom in Iraq was in the middle of a campaign against Article 79 of the Jaafari Personal Status Law—a law which, among other women's rights violations, would grant custody over any child two years or older to the father in divorce cases, lower the marriage age to nine for girls and 15 for boys, and even open the door for girls younger than nine to be married with a parent's approval. Now it takes everything the organization has just to keep their shelters open and women safe.

"We cannot speak of women's rights now unless we are speaking of the livelihood of those who are totally jeopardized, such as women who lost families and young girls who are vulnerable to corrupt officials or clerics," said Yanar Mohammad. "We went from legal work and improving rights of women to working in a state of emergency and trying to find the lowest chain in society and get them to safety."

The Tangled Web the U.S. Wove

Such extreme sectarian violence is a relatively new phenomenon in Iraq, reflects Yanar Mohammad, who is "sick and tired" of western pundits on TV saying there is no hope for Iraq.

"The mainstream media trashing Iraqi people is unbearable and is a total manipulation of the facts of America's role in dividing Iraqi people," said Yanar Mohammad. "The political process that the U.S. government put in place is a total failure and they [the United States] just left. The damage is not on them, it's on us now."

The damage comes in the form of, among other things, a generation that didn't have access to education.

"This generation listens to whatever the clerics and politicians say," said Yanar Mohammad. "They are ready to throw themselves in the fire and they do it in the name of their Imam. . . . Both politicians and religious heads are pushing the country into a very sectarian divide and it's frightening."

Christian women in the areas controlled by ISIS are forced to wear [the] hijab or face death.

Refugees Flee to Kurdish Region

As the fighting intensifies in northern and western Iraq, over 300,000 people have already fled to the Kurdish region for safety, where the United Nations and relief organizations have set up a refugee camp in the arid region of Khazer.

"It is very hot and there is no water; we were not prepared for this influx of refugees," says a Global Fund ally in Erbil, the capital of Iraqi Kurdistan. "The situation is by no means sustainable. The majority has nowhere to go and is staying in parks. Entire families are left without the most basic of shelter, food, and clothes."

While these waves of displacement to Kurdistan include Shia, Sunni, and Christian families, the pressure on Iraqi Christians has been strongest due to the infamous brutality of ISIS.

"Christian women in the areas controlled by ISIS are forced to wear hijab or face death," said a Global Fund ally who lives in Baghdad. "They must pay a protection tax, or *jizyah* to ISIS to stay safe."

If the violence is not seriously addressed, our ally in Erbil says Iraqi women know exactly what is going to happen next because they have endured it over and over again since the U.S. invasion in 2003, and during the first and second Gulf War.

"We know what has happened to women in Iraq—a lot of murders and violations—and we have already suffered to an unbearable extent," said the Global Fund ally in Erbil. "There is nothing they haven't done to us, which is why panic spreads among women as soon as we hear of another crisis. Women are used as a weapon for retaliation."

Turkey's Rampant Domestic Violence Problem

Emily Feldman

Emily Feldman is a journalist living in Istanbul, Turkey.

Residents of an upscale Istanbul neighborhood flocked to their windows this month [July 2014] to watch a neighbor brutally beat his wife. One onlooker—a European woman—recounted the woman's screams and her neighbors' apathy in a post to an Istanbul Facebook group.

"I asked one of the neighbors to call the police but she refused and continued watching, like it was a soap opera," the woman wrote. "It seems violence is a normal thing here, and nobody cares!!"

Violence Against Women in Turkey

The post generated more than 100 comments, many from fellow Westerners who said that they too had been disturbed by violent scenes they couldn't imagine unfolding back home: diners and waitstaff politely ignoring a man slapping his date in the face; pedestrians strolling past a public assault on a woman; a shopkeeper shrugging off a news report about a man slicing his wife's nose off her face. "That's Turkey," a woman recalled the vendor saying.

Violence against women is a pervasive problem in Turkey that affects nearly 40 percent of the country's female population, according to a widely cited 2009 study. It is behind 20 percent of divorces, according to a recent government survey, and has claimed at least 120 lives since January 1 alone, an increase from the same period last year, according to several

Emily Feldman, "Turkey's Rampant Domestic Violence Problem," *Daily Beast*, July 18, 2014. Copyright © 2014 The Daily Beast. All rights reserved. Reproduced with permission.

Turkish NGOs and data from Bianet, a news site that tallies killings reported in the media. It spans class and location, even making its way onto mainstream TV, as it did in May when a dating game show contestant revealed, on air, that he had killed his wife and later axed his lover to death.

Turkey's political system is overwhelmingly male, with women accounting for just 14 percent of the seats in parliament and an even smaller sliver of local government positions.

Turkey's chronic domestic violence was among the frustrations that prompted a group of women's rights activists—seven women and two men—to escalate their fight for gender equality last month by launching what could become the country's first-ever women's political party to participate in general elections.

The Women's Party

The founding members of Kadin Partisi, or Women's Party, reasoned the country was in need of a radical cultural shift that would only happen with more women in positions of power. As traditional activists, they could only do so much— aid women after they had been beaten; fight discriminatory policies after they had been written; offer advice and hope it might be heeded. But a party that could fill the seats of government with women, they believe, could finally balance a masculine culture that permeates the rest of the country.

"We are 50 percent of the population," Fusun Yurtman, a founding board member, said in an interview with *The Daily Beast.* "Yet males are making decisions about women's issues from the moment they're born. Even from conception," she added, referring to government attempts to limit access to abortions.

Turkey's political system is overwhelmingly male, with women accounting for just 14 percent of the seats in parliament and an even smaller sliver of local government positions, according to data from Kader, a group that tracks women's participation in politics. Men also dominate the judiciary and police force—which should be strong lines of defense for victims of domestic violence, but which critics instead characterize as boys' clubs that go easy on men when it comes to "family disputes."

"The problem is in the application, the interpretation of law," said Fatma Aytac, another founding member, adding that cops and courts tend to view men as the head of the family and take their word over their wives'. "Police come from this culture. Everyone comes from this culture."

The Prime Minister

The party also points a reproachful finger at Turkey's populist prime minister, Recep Tayyip Erdogan, for perpetuating the country's machismo through routine off-the-cuff morality rants: about how abortion is murder, C-sections are unnatural, co-ed dorms are breeding grounds for vice, and how every woman should have three children. These statements, the party founders say, serve as a disturbing model for Erdogan supporters, whether his opinions find their way into policy or not.

Whatever Erdogan's influence on Turkey's masculine culture may be, the country's gender fault lines long predate his time in power. Domestic violence, for example, has provided thematic fodder for generations of writers and filmmakers. Turkish author Elif Shafak begins her novel *Honor*, a story about women murdered for shaming their families, with a childhood memory about a neighbor who beat his wife. "In the evenings we listened to the shouts, the cries, the swearing. In the morning we went on with our lives as usual. The entire neighborhood pretended not to have heard, not to have seen."

More recently, however, Shafak has expressed optimism about a growing grassroots movement in Turkey to acknowledge and end violence against women. "More and more public figures are coming out to say that domestic violence is everyone's business and we should, as a society, interfere," she wrote in a 2011 *Guardian* article.

The founders of Kadin Partisi ... see women in male-dominant political parties as subordinate to the parties' masculine agendas.

Zeynep Kandur, who works for the women's branch of Erdogan's Justice and Development Party, has also observed many improvements over the years. "Twenty years ago you wouldn't report domestic violence," she said. "You wouldn't tell your own mother-in-law." Through the bleakness of rising domestic violence statistics, she sees a positive sign: More women and families are now reporting these sorts of crimes rather than sweeping them under the rug.

She also defends Erdogan against accusations of machismo, arguing that he has consistently pushed for more women in the party and that, since he took power in 2003, female representation in parliament has increased from 4 to 14 percent.

The Party's Agenda

The founders of Kadin Partisi, however, see women in male-dominant political parties as subordinate to the parties' masculine agendas. "They apply the parties' policies, they collect the votes for men," Yurtman said.

The Women's Party itself, the founders point out, does not plan to simply turn the tables and exclude men from their agenda. While boosting female representation in politics is a top priority, the party bills itself as a body striving for universal equality and eager to fight discrimination in any form.

To realize their vision, the party will first have to raise enough money to build branches across the country—a necessity if they want a shot at participating in next year's parliamentary elections. A pioneering women's party established in Turkey in the 1970s failed to cross this critical threshold.

On a recent sweltering Thursday afternoon several founders hunched over a table brainstorming how to do exactly that. They had launched too late to prepare for the country's August presidential elections—which Erdogan is expected to win, extending his influence for at least another five years—but were optimistic, looking ahead to 2015.

They said they had been well received by women on visits throughout the country and they reasoned that if they could get just one supporter per household, they'd be in business. "We can easily convince them," Aytac said.

Organizations to Contact

The editors have compiled the following list of organizations concerned with the issues debated in this book. The descriptions are derived from materials provided by the organizations. All have publications or information available for interested readers. The list was compiled on the date of publication of the present volume; names, addresses, phone and fax numbers, and e-mail and Internet addresses may change. Be aware that many organizations take several weeks or longer to respond to inquiries, so allow as much time as possible.

FaithTrust Institute
2900 Eastlake Ave. E., Suite 200, Seattle, WA   98102
(206) 634-1903 • fax: (206) 634-0115
website: www.faithtrustinstitute.org

FaithTrust Institute is a national, multifaith, multicultural training and education organization working to end sexual and domestic violence around the globe. FaithTrust Institute offers a wide range of services and resources, including training, consulting, and educational materials. The organization publishes many articles, including "A Perspective on Domestic Violence in the Muslim Community."

Human Rights Watch (HRW)
350 Fifth Ave., 34th Floor, New York, NY   10118-3299
(212) 290-4700 • fax: (212) 736-1300
e-mail: hrwnyc@hrw.org
website: www.hrw.org

Human Rights Watch (HRW) is dedicated to protecting the human rights of people around the world. HRW investigates human rights abuses, educates the public, and works to change policy and practice. Among its numerous publications is the report "'Here, Rape is Normal': A Five-Point Plan to Curtail Sexual Violence in Somalia."

INCITE!

2416 W. Victory Blvd., Burbank, CA   91506
e-mail: incite.natl@gmail.com
website: www.incite-national.org

INCITE! is a national activist organization of radical feminists of color advancing a movement to end violence against women of color through direct action, critical dialogue, and grassroots organizing. INCITE! works with groups and communities to develop political projects that address the multiple forms of violence women of color experience. INCITE! has several books, posters, and articles available at its website.

Legal Momentum

5 Hanover Square, Suite 1502, New York, NY   10014
(212) 925-6635
e-mail: peo@legalmomentum.org
website: www.legalmomentum.org

Legal Momentum is the nation's oldest legal defense and education fund dedicated to advancing the rights of all women and girls. Legal Momentum works to advance these rights through litigation and public policy advocacy, helping to pass the federal Violence Against Women Act. Legal Momentum publishes numerous reports and has links to articles written by its staff at their website.

National Coalition Against Domestic Violence (NCADV)

2000 M St. NW, Suite 480, Washington, DC   20036
(202) 467-8714
e-mail: publicpolicy@ncadv.org
website: www.ncadv.org

The National Coalition Against Domestic Violence (NCADV) works to raise awareness about domestic violence and to support those impacted by domestic violence. The NCADV Public Policy Office collaborates with other national organizations to promote legislation and policies that serve and protect victims and survivors of domestic violence. NCADV publishes numerous fact sheets and reports at its website, including "Guns and Domestic Violence."

National Coalition For Men (NCFM)
932 C St., Suite B, San Diego, CA   92101
(888) 223-1280
e-mail: ncfm@ncfm.org
website: www.ncfm.org

The National Coalition For Men (NCFM) is a nonprofit educational organization that aims to raise awareness about the ways sex discrimination affects men and boys. NCFM uses activism through its many chapters to end sex discrimination. NCFM publishes *Transitions: Journal of Men's Perspectives.*

National Network to End Domestic Violence (NNEDV)
1400 16th St. NW, Suite 330, Washington, DC   20036
(202) 543-5566 • fax: (202) 543-5626
website: www.nnedv.org

The National Network to End Domestic Violence (NNEDV) is a social change organization dedicated to creating a social, political, and economic environment in which violence against women no longer exists. NNEDV works to address and respond to needs identified by victims by providing tools that strengthen advocacy and help change the way society responds to domestic violence. NNEDV has a variety of publications and other information available at its website.

National Organization for Women (NOW)
1100 H St. NW, 3rd Floor, Washington, DC   20005
(202) 628-8669 • fax: (202) 785-8576
website: www.now.org

The National Organization for Women (NOW) is the largest organization of feminist activists in the United States working to take action to bring about equality for all women. NOW works to eliminate discrimination and harassment in the workplace, schools, the justice system, and all other sectors of society; secure abortion, birth control and reproductive rights for all women; end all forms of violence against women; eradicate racism, sexism and homophobia; and promote equality and justice in our society. NOW has many publications available at its website, including the issue advisory "Will Military Sexual Assault Survivors Find Justice?"

National Sexual Violence Resource Center (NSVRC)
123 North Enola Dr., Enola, PA   17025
(877) 739-3895 • fax: (717) 909-0714
website: www.nsvrc.org

The National Sexual Violence Resource Center (NSVRC) aims to provide leadership in preventing and responding to sexual violence. NSVRC acts as a communication hub connecting people with the information, resources, tools, and expertise needed to effectively address and prevent sexual violence in all communities. NSVRC publishes fact sheets, booklets, articles, and issue briefs, including "Young Men of Color and the Other Side of Harm: Addressing Disparities in Our Responses to Violence."

Office on Violence Against Women
145 N St. NE, Suite 10W.121, Washington, DC   20530
(202) 307-6026 • fax: (202) 305-2589
e-mail: ovw.info@usdoj.gov
website: www.justice.gov/ovw

The Office on Violence Against Women (OVW), a component of the US Department of Justice, provides federal leadership in developing the national capacity to reduce violence against women. OVW administers justice for and strengthens services to victims of domestic violence, dating violence, sexual assault, and stalking. OVW publishes several reports annually, which are available at its website.

Stop Abusive and Violent Environments (SAVE)
PO Box 1221, Rockville, MD   20849
(301) 801-0608
e-mail: info@saveservices.org
website: www.saveservices.org

Stop Abusive and Violent Environments (SAVE) is a victim-advocacy organization working for legal reform. SAVE sponsors victims, survivors, and persons falsely accused of abuse or sexual assault, aiming to strengthen due process and keep the presumption of innocence. SAVE publishes a variety of reports, which are available at its website.

Bibliography

Books

Jimmy Carter	*A Call to Action: Women, Religion, Violence, and Power.* New York: Simon & Schuster, 2014.
Walter S. DeKeseredy	*Violence Against Women: Myths, Facts, Controversies.* Toronto: University of Toronto Press, 2011.
R. Emerson Dobash and Russell P. Dobash	*When Men Murder Women.* New York: Oxford University Press, 2015.
Elizabeth Gerhardt	*The Cross and Gendercide: A Theological Response to Global Violence Against Women and Girls.* Downers Grove, IL: Inter Varsity Press, 2014.
Carol Jordan	*Violence Against Women in Kentucky: A History of US and State Legislative Reform.* Lexington: University Press of Kentucky, 2014.
Mary P. Koss, Jacquelyn W. White, and Alan E. Kazdin, eds.	*Violence Against Women and Children: Navigating Solutions.* Washington, DC: American Psychological Association, 2011.
Laura La Bella	*Dating Violence.* New York: Rosen Publishing, 2015.
Nancy Lombard	*Young People's Understandings of Men's Violence Against Women.* Burlington, VT: Ashgate, 2015.

Dorothy E. McBride and Janine A. Parry	*Women's Rights in the USA: Policy Debates and Gender Roles.* New York: Routledge, 2011.
Michael A. Messner and Max A. Greenberg	*Some Men: Feminist Allies and the Movement to End Violence Against Women.* Boulder, CO: Paradigm Publishers, 2015.
David L. Richards and Jillienne Haglund	*Violence Against Women and the Law.* Boulder, CO: Paradigm Publishers, 2015.
Beth Richie	*Arrested Justice: Black Women, Violence, and America's Prison Nation.* New York: New York University Press, 2012.
Christina Hoff Sommers	*The War Against Boys: How Misguided Policies Are Harming Our Young Men.* New York: Simon & Schuster, 2013.
Mary White Stewart	*Ordinary Violence: Everyday Assaults Against Women Worldwide.* Santa Barbara, CA: Praeger, 2014.
Jacqui True	*The Political Economy of Violence Against Women.* New York: Oxford University Press, 2012.

Periodicals and Internet Sources

Molly Ball	"Why Would Anyone Oppose the Violence Against Women Act?," *Atlantic*, February 12, 2013.

Max Baucus	"Work Is Not Done to Combat Domestic Violence," *U.S. News & World Report*, March 19, 2012.
Joe Biden	"The Hard Fight to End Violence Against Women," *News Journal* (Delaware), September 7, 2014.
Rosa Brooks	"Is Sexual Assault Really an 'Epidemic'?," *Foreign Policy*, July 10, 2013.
Mona Charen	"Campus Rape Is Real," *National Review*, December 5, 2014.
Hannah Chartoff	"The Root of India's Domestic Violence and Son Preference," Council on Foreign Relations, February 2, 2015. www.cfr.org.
Janice Shaw Crouse	"The Violence Against Women Act Should Outrage Decent People," *U.S. News & World Report*, March 19, 2012.
Robert Franklin	"VAWA Must Be Reformed for Domestic Violence Rates to Come Down," *The Hill*, February 4, 2013.
Charlotte Hays	"Violence Against Numbers," Independent Women's Forum, February 1, 2012. www.iwf.org.
Lisalyn R. Jacobs	"Women: When We Succeed, We Can Also Escape Abuse," *Women's e-News*, March 13, 2014. www.womensenews.org.

Wendy Kaminer — "What's Wrong with the Violence Against Women Act," *Atlantic*, March 19, 2012.

Caroline Kitchens — "It's Time to End 'Rape Culture' Hysteria," *Time*, March 20, 2014.

Sarah Lazare — "Military Sexual Assault and Rape 'Epidemic,'" *Al Jazeera*, October 20, 2011. www.aljazeera.com.

Zerlina Maxwell — "Rape Culture Is Real," *Time*, March 27, 2014.

Miriam Zoila Pérez — "Seven Important Facts About the Violence Against Women Act at 20," *Colorlines*, September 12, 2014. www.colorlines.com.

Julie Pollak — "What Politicians Don't Say About the Military's Sexual Assault 'Epidemic,'" *Breitbart*, November 4, 2013. www.breitbart.com.

Meghan Rhoad — "Addressing Violence Against All Women," *The Hill*, April 20, 2012.

Lindsay L. Rodman — "The Pentagon's Bad Math on Sexual Assault," *Wall Street Journal*, May 19, 2013.

Eryn Sepp — "Service, Not Subservience: The U.S. Military's Sexual-Violence Problem," *Daily Beast*, March 8, 2013. www.thedailybeast.com.

Tierney Sneed "Ray Rice Is a Reminder Why Congress Passed the Violence Against Women Act," *U.S. News & World Report*, September 9, 2014.

Christina Hoff Sommers "The Media Is Making College Rape Culture Worse," *Daily Beast*, January 23, 2015. www.thedailybeast.com.

Luigi Spinola and Preethi Nallu "Violence Against Women and Gang Rape: India's Continuing Shame," *Newsweek*, February 14, 2014. www.newsweek.com.

Salamishah Tillet "The Fake Violence Against Women Act," *Nation*, May 17, 2012.

Jessica Valenti "America's Rape Problem: We Refuse to Admit That There Is One," *Nation*, January 4, 2013.

Christina Villegas "Does VAWA Foster Class Victimization Among Women?," Independent Women's Forum, July 17, 2012. www.iwf.org.

Peter Westmacott and Melanne Verveer "War's Silent Scourge: Sexual Violence Against Women," *Daily Beast*, November 25, 2012. www.thedailybeast.com.

Laura Wood "Violence Against Women Act Is a Totalitarian Violation of Democracy," *U.S. News & World Report*, March 19, 2012.

Emily Yoffe "The College Rape Overcorrection," *Slate*, December 7, 2014. www.slate.com.

Index

Prison Rape Elimination Act
  (2003), 130
Protect Our Defenders, 79
public awareness campaigns, 127

R

Radwan, Zahra, 164–167
Rahman, Mujibur, 149
Ramirez, Gloria Inés, 158
rape crimes. *See also* Gang rape;
  Violence against women during
  war
    male rape, 18–24
    mass psychology of rape, 100–
      103
    reporting rates for, 112–113
    spousal rape, 120
    stranger rape, 115, 120
rape culture
    epidemic as fiction, 53–57
    as hoax, 58–60
    need for safety, 47–48
    patriarchal society as cause,
      97–103
    reality of, 44–48
    reassessment of, 62–63
    sexual assault statistics, 60–62
    skepticism over, 44–45, 53–57,
      58–63
    toxic masculinity, 91–96
Reagan, David, 37
Renda, Emily, 62
Revolutionary United Front
  (RUF), 149
Rice, Ray, 118
Rich, Adrienne, 98
Ringle, Ken, 50
Ripley, Katherine, 60
Rita, Ana, 159

Robert F. Kennedy journalism
  award, 74
Rolling Stone magazine, 45, 58, 60
Rosen, Ruth, 121–125
Rubio, Olga Victoria, 156–157
Runaway and Homeless Youth Act,
  107
Rwandan genocide, 143, 148–151
Rwandan Patriotic Front, 148

S

Safe Start Initiative provides, 131
Santilli, Pete, 82
SAVE (Stop Abusive and Violent
  Environments), 135–136
Sclove, Lena, 62
sectarian violence, 165–166
Sellers, Bakari, 41
Senate Armed Services Commit-
  tee, 80
Services, Training, Officers, and
  Prosecutors Violence Against
  Women (STOP) grants, 129, 130
sex jihad, 164
sex scandals in government, 78–83
sex selection concerns, 161–162
sexual assault/violence. *See also*
  Rape crimes; Rape culture; Vio-
  lence against women
    defined, 15
    by gender and race, 18–25
    impact of, 29–30
    incidence of, 28–29
    intimate partner violence,
      22–25
    overview, 18
    prevalence of, 18–22
    statistics, 60–62
sexual coercion, 19, 21

CPSIA information can be obtained
at www.ICGtesting.com
Printed in the USA
FFOW05n2005141215

9 780737 774276